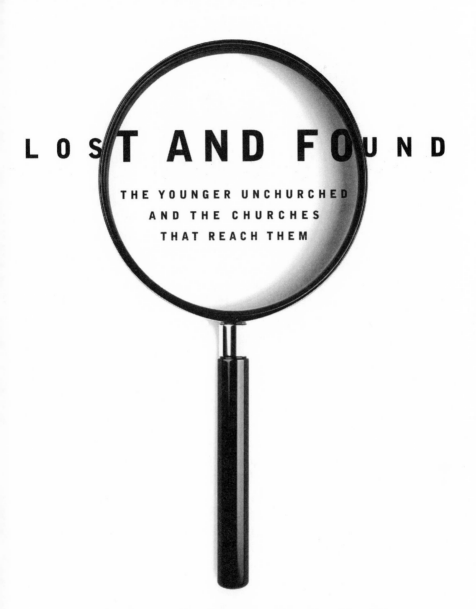

LOST AND FOUND

THE YOUNGER UNCHURCHED
AND THE CHURCHES
THAT REACH THEM

ED STETZER
RICHIE STANLEY AND JASON HAYES

B&H
PUBLISHING GROUP

NASHVILLE, TENNESSEE

978-0-8054-4878-8

Published by B&H Publishing Group,
Nashville, Tennessee

Dewey Decimal Classification: 269.2
Subject Heading: EVANGELISTIC WORK \ NON-CHURCH-
AFFILIATED PEOPLE \ YOUNG ADULTS

1 2 3 4 5 6 7 8 9 10 • 13 12 11 10 09

CONTENTS

INTRODUCTION

WE'VE ALL DONE IT—MISPLACED AN IMPORTANT SET OF KEYS, a cell phone, a watch, or maybe even an iPod. It's always frustrating, and if we get really desperate, some of us even pray that God would help us find what we have lost! We also know the excitement of finding a valuable item we had lost. That's why we are writing this book. Many in this generation are unchurched, and we want to help the church find and reach these lost young people.

After all, Jesus came to seek and to save those who are lost, not just point out how bad it was that people are lost. He told parables about a lost sheep, a lost coin, and a lost son. In those stories He also pointed out how excited heaven gets when lost people are found.

Much has been written and said about younger adults and their view of church. You don't need a lot of research to tell you what you already know. Young adults (and some who care about them) have been swinging away at the church like it was a low-hanging piñata.

But this book is not entitled *Lost and We Just Wanted to Tell You (and it's the church's fault, by the way)*. We're calling it *Lost and Found* because we want you to know that lost young adults are being found—effectively engaged in their culture, coming to faith in Christ, and being incorporated into congregational life.

In this book you will find research and stories about unchurched younger adults. But we're going to give you more than that. You also will hear from churches that are effectively reaching unchurched younger adults.

The book has three sections. The first section looks at the "who." Who are younger adults today? What do they look like? What do they think about God, Christianity, and the church? We will explore some of the overlap that occurs between the younger unchurched and their dissatisfied younger churched counterparts. But our main focus will be on the unchurched.

Based on additional research, the second section provides a thorough analysis of the ministry needs of the younger unchurched.

The third and final section looks at churches that are reaching young adults, with a focus that combines the who and the how. We will examine churches that are effectively engaging emerging culture and regularly seeing young adults come to faith in Christ. Instead of telling you what you should do, we analyze churches that are doing it—and we seek to learn from them.

What This Book Is Not

This is not a book about young adult church dropouts. Read Thom and Sam Rainer's *Essential Church* for an informative look at this issue.

This is not a book on the emerging, contemporary, or reformed movements that have reached many young adults. However, church examples of all three movements can be found in the later chapters of this book.

Finally, this is not a prescriptive book with magical answers to the problems plaguing churches devoid of young adults. Each church we profile, like yours, is unique in its setting, ministry, and calling.

Where Did We Find the Data?

This book is basically a report on three different research projects. First, a series of polls was undertaken by the Center for Missional Research at the North American Mission Board and LifeWay Research from 2006 to 2008. Richie Stanley leads that team, and he has provided important insights throughout the book.

Second, LifeWay undertook a large study of young adults starting in 2005 as part of the Threads initiative. As part of that research, we contacted young adults and did nearly 800 total surveys (254 ministry leaders, 271 churched, 272 unchurched) and nearly 100 face-to-face interviews. Jason was part of that research and is now a leading part of that initiative. That's one reason I asked him to coauthor the book with me.

Third, we surveyed 149 churches that were reaching an extraordinary number of young adults. Then we conducted telephone interviews with fifty specific churches to see if we could identify any trends among them. The mix of churches from multidenominations (or none at all) gives an eye-opening look at the best practices of churches reaching young adults. We did not want to ask just anyone what they thought about how to reach emerging generations, so we actually asked those who were reaching them—crazy idea, I know, but it made sense to us.

Our Bias

This is a book about who the younger unchurched are and how to reach them. Yes, that may be a little old school. Many authors and speakers want to focus on fascinating and important questions like what is wrong with our belief system, how can we do this differently, and what will the future look like for churches? I have asked questions like that myself, and I will do more of that in my next book. But, in this book, Richie, Jason, and I are asking one simple question: Who are the young unchurched and how can they be reached with the good news of Jesus Christ? (OK, that's two questions.)

We are unapologetic about this. A movement may be emerging, contemporary, reformed, or whatever, but if it fails to produce new followers of Jesus Christ, it is only a fascinating and engaging dead end. This book is not focused on protest movements, Internet fads, or well-known speakers. We simply want to know who is reaching young adults and what we can learn from them.

Our Format

Throughout the book we write as a team. All of us have contributed to each part. However, to make it easier for you as you read, we will not use individual names unless absolutely necessary. Portions written in first person should be taken to be Ed's voice. When Richie or Jason is speaking, that will be indicated.

Also, you will follow a narrative throughout the first two parts of the book that concludes in the last chapter. The narrative is based on the four young adults you'll meet in chapter 1. The characteristics of each person are based on real demographics and trend information. The narrative takes real people and creates composite characters based on how young adults might look, interact, and relate in relationship to one another. Although the narrative is hypothetical, it certainly represents the lives of millions of twentysomethings.

The Situation

We also need to say up front a few things that are not true. We have heard them and guess you have too: "This will be the last Christian generation," "Only 4 percent of this generation are Christians," and "The sky is falling." Well, there are some concerns (and big ones at that), but hype does not help. Crises sell books but usually don't fix problems. However, real research shows the opportunities as well as the challenges.

The General Social Survey, a national survey conducted at least biannually since 1972, provides a snapshot as to how religious attendance among twentysomethings has changed over time. Looking at the full sample in the graph below, we can see that there has been a

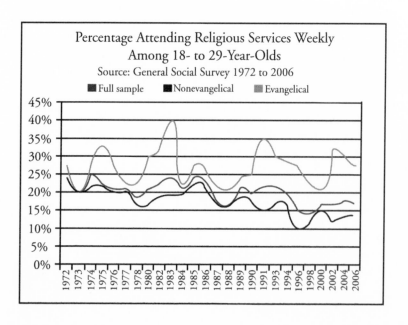

Percentage Attending Religious Services Weekly
Among 18- to 29-Year-Olds
Source: General Social Survey 1972 to 2006
■ Full sample   ■ Nonevangelical   ■ Evangelical

declining percentage of eighteen- to twenty-nine-year-olds attending a religious service weekly or more, with the lowest dip occurring in the mid 1990s. However, we can see the beginning of several upticks in the percentage attending weekly since the year 2000. Time will only tell if the current, rising trajectory will continue. In comparing evangelicals to nonevangelicals, we can see that both groups follow the general decrease over time, but each again with a recent upswing since 2000 (and some drop in evangelical attendance the last few years).

Keep in mind, the comparison of religious service attendance for eighteen- to twenty-nine-year-olds in 1972 with similarly aged cohorts after 2000 are not identical comparisons. The eighteen- to twenty-nine-year-old population in the 1970s were more likely to be married, more likely to have children, were less racially diverse, and were less college educated than the same age group in 2008. Robert Wuthnow of Princeton University in his book, *After the Baby Boomers,* comments on the general decline:

> There is no question that people attend religious services
> for religious reasons. Yet the likelihood of someone
> actually attending is undeniably conditioned by his or her
> circumstances. Statistical evidence identifies the broad
> contours of these circumstances. It matters especially for
> young adults if they are married or single, have children or
> do not have children, work outside the home or do not work,
> and so on. The precise reasons why these circumstances make
> the difference they do can be inferred from the patterns
> themselves. Married people, for instance, not only go to
> church more often than single people do, but have a more
> enduring relationship with a person of the opposite sex, have
> or anticipate having children to whom they must responsibly
> impart values, and have probably chosen a group of friends
> who lead lives similar to theirs.[1]

Wuthnow's study, among other things, also finds that although a general decline in religious attendance has occurred among American younger adults, other measures of belief and spirituality have not suffered such a decline. For instance, little change has occurred since the 1970s in the proportion of young adults who believe the Bible to be the Word of God. Wuthnow finds that a greater percentage of current young adults, compared to older adults, prefer personal experience as the best way to experience God. Wuthnow identifies current young adults as spiritual tinkerers rather than religious service attendees. He states:

> The overall conclusion from the evidence . . . is that spiritual tinkering is quite common among young adults of today and probably will remain so among young adults of tomorrow. This is because spiritual tinkering was not just a form of restlessness that characterized baby boomers and then could easily be reversed among their offspring. Spiritual tinkering is a reflection of the pluralistic religious society in which we live, the freedom we permit ourselves in making choices about faith, and the necessity of making those choices in the face of the uprootedness and change that most young adults experience.[2]

So, there are issues—big ones. But the faith has not been lost in one generation. Yet, increasingly, the trends are not good—which is why we wrote this book. Now, on to the book!

We realize you do not need another book of statistics. But what we do need is something to help all of us engage an increasingly lost generation with the gospel of Jesus Christ. We need tools that will help us seek and save those of this generation who are lost. As you read, our prayer is that you will be challenged to take action, so that the lost may be found.

— PART 1 —

Polling

TO STUDY THE YOUNGER UNCHURCHED IT IS IMPORTANT to talk to the younger unchurched. There are many opinions about the unchurched out there—much of it based on gut, some on conjecture, and some on anecdotal evidence. To understand people, we think you have to ask people. So, we polled them—more than a thousand of them.

We wanted to do something more than just ask young adults who are unchurched. We wanted to know how their views differed from the older unchurched. We believed it might help us understand something important: are their views more negative or more positive than their older counterparts? If so, that might help us understand what was happening—and we found some interesting things.

The polling section is broken into three parts:

Types of the Younger Unchurched

We began by describing some types of the younger unchurched. To be fair, every unchurched person is an individual. However, we have observed that not everyone is equally hostile, informed, or open. Thus, we described four types and created a narrative that continues throughout the book to help tell the story of these younger unchurched types.

What They Believe

The second section is straight polling. We developed a series of questions to survey these younger unchurched people and then asked them questions about spirituality, church, God, religion, and faith. The results were both fascinating and sobering.

What Does the Future Hold?

The third part of this section compares the younger unchurched to the older. The reason is simple. Amid much talk about this generation being so unchurched and lost, we need to ask, "Are they any different from the generation that proceeded them?" And, you might be surprised by the answer. We concluded that basic beliefs about God and their perceptions of the church would be worth discussing more in depth.

Types of the
Younger Unchurched

MOST PEOPLE DON'T LIKE IT WHEN THEY ARE NARROWLY DEFINED by the opinions and expectations of others. For example, it can be a mistake to put young people into one grouping and say, "All young adults think this or that." In our study we found remarkable differences by race, ethnicity, and background, among other things. Based on careful research, we found clear patterns that differentiated the younger unchurched, and we thought it would be helpful to describe those patterns.

So really, Younger Unchurched Al doesn't exist. As we talked to many younger unchurched adults, we found that they fit into several categories, but even these are imperfect. The younger unchurched expressed a desire for churches to care about them as individuals, so it is with great caution that we describe four general types of younger unchurched in this chapter. The intention is to learn about differences among the types rather than create stereotypes.

There certainly is some overlap to these categories, but the four general types of younger unchurched we described are:

1. Always unchurched (never been involved)
2. De-churched (having attended as a child)

3. Friendly unchurched (not particularly angry at the church)
4. Hostile unchurched (angry at the church or have had some
negative experiences with the church)

Always Unchurched

The always unchurched are those younger unchurched who either
reported that they never attended church as a child or attended only on
special occasions.

Meet Ally, a representative of the always unchurched. She is twenty-
five, has never married, and has a college degree. Ally grew up near a
large city and has never developed an identity with any denomination,
faith group, or spiritual support system. Ally represents about 22 percent of the younger unchurched in our sample.

Compared to other unchurched young people, she has the smallest, yet widest view of God and Jesus. Yes, God or a supreme being
probably exists, and this does somewhat impact her lifestyle. But the
God described in the Bible is not unique from the gods depicted by
other world religions such as Islam or Hinduism. Ally does not believe
that Jesus died and actually came back to life, yet she is open-minded
enough to admit that having faith in Jesus might make a positive difference in a person's life.

Christianity is so prevalent that it does seem to be a relevant and
viable religion for today. She believes Christian churches are probably even helpful to society as a whole. But Ally is convinced that
Christianity should focus more on loving God and people and less on
organizations.

Ally has no church experience, but she still believes many churchgoers are hypocritical in judging other people. Her lifestyle choices
would probably be judged harshly by the church, so why would she
desire to subject herself to that? Ally simply has no need for church
in her busy life. She can relate well to God and learn about being a
Christian without attending church.

Ally differs from her age group peers in several of her views about
the church and Christians. Ally is slightly less spiritual and religious
than other unchurched twentysomethings, but she is somewhat curious
about God, or a supreme being. Some of her friends are spiritual, and
she disagrees with the notion that church attendees are more spiritual
than she and her friends.

Ally seldom wonders about her eternal destiny because she is not at all certain that a person's spirit continues to exist after death. Heaven just might exist, but Ally is not really concerned about hell. Since her views of the afterlife are weak, they have relatively little impact on how she lives.

Ally's lack of church experience will make it difficult for existing churches or Christian acquaintances to reach her. As is true of all the younger unchurched, Ally would listen to believers who were willing to share with her about their Christian beliefs.

Like her peers, Ally has a good friend who is a Christian and knows several others. But they get on her nerves sometimes. Last year when Ally's friend Ann became a Christian, their relationship suffered.

Ally has indicated that she will not be attracted by a particular music style at church. She is ambivalent about churches caring for her as a person and sharing truth with her in relevant ways. She just has no comfort level at church. The potential benefits of church involvement do not outweigh the perceived negatives for her.

The De-Churched

We were surprised at how many of the younger unchurched indicated they had attended church as a child. For some, this childhood attendance seemed to be a negative experience. We looked at those who attended as a child and now thought the church was full of hypocrites. Our assumption was that many of these people had a bad experience in church—and therefore, they were *de*-churched.

To be fair, this category is probably overestimated—most people tend to report that they were involved in activities that society affirms (i.e., if you ask them if they voted in the last election, more say "yes" than actually voted). However, this group displays some characteristics that are interesting and helpful to know. An increasing number of studies show that people estimate their church attendance at twice the amount they actually attend—and this may be even higher if they are reflecting back on childhood.

Because the de-churched are the largest subgroup (62 percent of respondents), their responses are similar to the overall survey totals. Their interest and receptivity are generally higher than the other types of younger unchurched.

Dean is similar to his unchurched peers, and like many of them, he attended church weekly as a child. Even though he no longer attends, Dean's upbringing has influenced his understanding of God, Christianity, and church toward more traditional views.

Dean's agreement with God's existence and uniqueness is strong, but he still leaves open the possibility that supreme beings of other world religions may be similar to the biblical God. He was taught and accepts the bodily resurrection of Jesus as fact, and he is convinced that believing in Jesus makes a positive difference in one's life.

Dean's receptivity to Bible studies or conversations about Christianity is above average. The church still has work to do overcoming the negative feelings that Dean holds about hypocrites in the church. He also has personal lifestyle issues that make him wonder if he would be accepted at church.

Dean wonders occasionally about his eternal destiny, much more than Ally, his friend who never went to church as a child. He has little doubt that a person's spirit continues postmortem, and he is more comfortable with the notion of heaven than hell. His lifestyle is impacted to some degree by his beliefs about the afterlife.

Dean knows many Christians and is open to spiritual discussion with them. He finds that some Christians do get on his nerves. His friendships are not limited to those who are spiritual, and church attendance does not convince Dean that a person is more spiritual than he is. After all, he indicates weekly that church attendance is not required for a person to have a good relationship with God and an understanding of Christianity.

Dean looks and thinks like the typical twentysomething not in church. It will not be easier to reach Dean than it will be to reach Ally, even though he is formerly churched, but it will help some. The big question is—where and how would Dean fit in if he came back?

Friendly and Hostile Unchurched

Friend or foe? The last two types of younger unchurched respondents are best viewed in contrast. On the one hand, 15 percent of the younger unchurched attended church weekly as a child and have no current animosity toward the church. The "friendly" unchurched do not view the church as a bunch of hypocrites, and Christians do not get on their nerves. This group is a subset of the de-churched younger population. Aaron will represent this group.

On the other hand, 37 percent of the younger unchurched are hostile toward the church and Christians. Regardless of their childhood experiences, this group agrees that hypocrites fill the pews and that Christians can often be annoying. Jacob will represent this group.

Choosing masculine names has no particular significance, as both genders are equally represented in each type of the younger unchurched.

Aaron and Jacob are on opposite ends of the receptivity scale among the younger unchurched. Aaron is not angry with the church. With his background of church attendance and friendly disposition, it almost seems accidental that he is not in church. Jacob, on the other hand, is anti-church and probably considers the church and her members to be bigoted and dangerous.

It is likely that Aaron's theology and views toward the church are more favorable than many who attend. In his mid-twenties, Aaron strongly agrees that God exists and is unique. While Jacob is less certain about God's existence, he flat out disagrees that the God described in the Bible is the only god. Jacob believes that the biblical God is the same as those presented by non-Christian religions.

While Jacob's hostility is primarily focused on the church, he also holds lower views of Jesus. He is ambivalent about the resurrection, though he reluctantly admits that believing in Jesus may have positive effects. Aaron, on the other hand, is very comfortable with Jesus' resurrection.

Aaron's affinity toward the church of his childhood is born out in his agreement that Christianity is relevant today and that the church is helpful to society. Neither of these notions resonates with Jacob.

So why is Aaron not attending? He is quite sure that it is not necessary to attend church in order to relate well with God, and he does not require instructions regarding Christianity from the church. Jacob's animosity toward the church is set off if anyone suggests that he needs the church for either relationship or instruction.

Since both Jacob and Aaron are interested in knowing more about God, each considers himself to be spiritual. Aaron is much more religious than his peers, and he may even identify with the denomination of his childhood. Jacob's hostility allows him no affinity toward any denomination or faith group.

Aaron still remembers being taught about heaven, and he wonders about his eternal destination occasionally. He believes strongly that heaven and hell both exist, and Aaron lives his life with that in mind. Jacob's lack of certainty about the afterlife, especially punishment, has much less impact on his lifestyle.

Anger is part of Jacob's response to the church, and he has no doubt that the church is all about organized religion instead of loving God and people. Both believe that Christianity is still a relevant religion, but even Aaron has concerns about the church organization taking priority over people.

Aaron is much more open to a small group study where he could learn about the Bible and Jesus. Jacob hates that idea. Familiar music at church would have some appeal for Aaron. Both Jacob and Aaron would appreciate a church that cared about them as persons.

A church that wants to reach Jacob with the gospel is going to have to do so on his turf, because Jacob is not coming to church. Aaron may respond to an appropriate invitation to church, especially from a friend.

These findings reveal some big implications for the church. For many, church evangelism has been focused on "bringing friends to church." That won't happen with Jacob or Ally. It might with Aaron and Dean. However, it is essential that churches focus on more than invitations. Further, the focus also needs to be incarnational—going and living among people who are far from God. Effective evangelistic outreach will not be a "one size fits all" approach.

The Younger Unchurched and Cultural Issues

Before we leave the polling research, it might be helpful to look at two more issues. Areas of controversy certainly exist within our culture that have an impact on how the unchurched view the church and its response to certain issues.

In the survey the unchurched twentysomethings were asked what impact two stances by a church would have on them. First they were asked, "If you were considering visiting or joining a church, would knowing that the church did not endorse the ordination of women as pastors negatively or positively impact your decision?"

Sixty-five percent of all the younger unchurched said this would negatively impact their decision. Only 6 percent said that this would be a positive. So, the negatives outnumbered the positives ten to one. (Almost 30 percent of respondents either said that the stance against women's ordination would not make a difference or that they were not sure.) The only major difference among the four types of unchurched were the friendly unchurched, and even 47 percent of them said this stance would negatively impact their decision to visit or join a church.

Another question was asked, "If you were considering visiting or joining a church, would knowing that the church did not welcome and affirm homosexual members negatively or positively impact your decision?" Once again the overwhelming majority of the younger unchurched reported this would negatively impact their decision. The range of responses by type—83 percent of the always unchurched and 52 percent of the friendly unchurched—indicates that each type would react negatively to a church that does not affirm homosexuals as members.

Certainly these are controversial issues and we have strong beliefs about them. Yet, you cannot have a serious conversation about reaching the unchurched, particularly the younger unchurched, without addressing issues of gender and sexuality. Later in the book, we will share details of how churches have dealt with and worked through these issues.

— A LOST AND FOUND STORY —

Mitch Phillips lowered his head over his bass guitar and chuckled at the site of Aaron's contorted face as he bent the strings of his sunburst Stratocaster, holding a note so long Mitch thought the strings would break. The crowd loved it; they always did. There are times Mitch is convinced Aaron believes he is the second coming of Eric Clapton, Kenny Wayne Shepherd, or Derek Trucks—and some nights he is close—but most nights the two of them realized their little band is lucky to land some semi-consistent gigs here at the Cozy Note doing covers of everything from Clapton to Coldplay.

In some ways Mitch wondered if this wasn't their way of hanging on to cool, at least in their minds. As they saw it, they were hip musicians on an occasional Friday and Saturday night. But would the occasional autograph seeker ask for a signed coaster if she knew Mitch had been a finance major, managed 401ks during the week, and drove the same Honda Accord he'd been driving since high school; or that Aaron taught high school English in the 'burbs and was a faculty sponsor for the yearbook staff? At the same time, it didn't matter to him if she would. At twenty-six and single, he knew Aaron and him at best probably only had a few more years playing together before life's reality finally overtook them.

Mitch still remembers the day they met six years earlier when they were both twenty and beginning their junior year. It was late August, and he'd just dropped his stuff in his dorm room when he heard familiar blues riffs ricocheting off the white cinder block walls. The sound pulled him up a stairwell and dragged him down the hall to an open door where he found

Aaron sitting on his amp and wearing a pair of sunglasses and head-phones. He was playing along with an old Allman Brothers song, but all that could be heard was Aaron's playing. Mitch raced back to his room—"Forget the unpacking," he thought—and grabbed his bass. A friendship was born, a band blossomed, and they eventually picked up some spare change playing frat parties.

Mitch's interest in music began ten years earlier when his parents began attending a new church. He didn't recall a word the preacher said from back then, because he couldn't take his eyes off the band. He loved music and the guitar player was phenomenal. James had been a studio player for years and noticed an enraptured Mitch dragging his parents every week to the band's side of the theatre where the church met.

"Do you play?" James asked one Sunday.

"No, but I'd love to learn," replied Mitch, somewhat embarrassed his admiration had been so obvious.

"Have you heard about the music club the church has?" asked James. "I teach in it as well as the other guys in the band. We have another session starting up. You don't need anything to get started. We've got some extra guitars, not great, but good enough to learn on. All I ask is that you commit to show up for the lessons and to practice. How 'bout it?"

"How 'bout it?" Mitch thought. It was a chance of a lifetime. He became a sponge and learned all he could. James became like a much older brother, inviting Mitch to studio sessions, and he even gave Mitch a slightly used Gibson acoustic guitar. The relationship grew, and James began to challenge Mitch about real life issues—girls, education, his relationship to Christ, life goals. Mitch had always been a good student and a good kid, but no one had ever confronted him with spiritual things. To be honest, he'd never given them much thought, but over time he couldn't get away from James's explanation of why he needed to ask Jesus into his heart. He put his trust in Christ midway through his junior year of college.

It was about that time the band's bass player had a job transfer, and they needed somebody to fill his place. Mitch volunteered, having goofed around with a bass off and on as he and James played. It came easier to him than the guitar, so he stuck with it. By the time he and Aaron connected he could hold his own. He and Aaron's friendship grew based on mutual respect for each other's musical ability.

But that was about all the two had in common. Mitch was a whiz at math and finished near the top of his high school class. Aaron was an average student who enjoyed art, literature, and music. He didn't necessarily want to be a teacher, but he saw having summers off as an opportunity to concentrate on music with an eye toward playing full time. Mitch was good with money and often found himself coaching fellow students out of a financial pit. It turned into a career. Aaron can't remember the last time his checkbook balanced, and in college often asked Mitch for advice—still does.

Mitch is serious about his Christianity and has grown in his theological understanding. Aaron went to church as a kid for a short time and periodically contemplates God, heaven and hell, his life, and why bad things happen to good people, but rarely are they deep thoughts. Music is his spiritual connection to God and he believes played with feeling and expression, music is a prayer. If people enjoy how you play, "music is a ministry to weary souls who forget about their troubles for a while," Aaron often tells Mitch.

"If that were the case," Mitch thinks as Aaron finally releases the note and turns his licks toward the song's end, "Aaron would be a high priest of soul salve tonight."

Just then Mitch catches Ally's wave as she and Dean break from the shadows and cigarette smoke to find their way to the "friends" table near the stage. He knew they'd make it. He knew they'd be late. Mitch glanced at his watch, shook his head and chuckled. He couldn't remember a single occasion when she'd been on time for their meetings at Starbucks.

What They Believe

WE HAVE HEARD IT AS MANY TIMES AS YOU HAVE—YOUNG adults are not connecting with the church. And it's true. Some make alarming statements like "Christianity will die out in this generation," and those make good conference promos. But it never helps the situation. Christianity will not die out in this generation or any other, but this generation is not connecting well to the current expression of Christianity. And that should concern us.

As Christians, showing and sharing the good news of Jesus is central to our call. Christianity is, by nature, a missionary faith. Much to the chagrin of many outside the church (and a few inside), we have been told to go and tell—and when we tell, we are to tell people how to become followers of Jesus.

So, how do you tell? What is the best way? Well, if you were a missionary to the Khosa (a South African tribe), you would study every aspect of their lives. You would learn their language, understand their worldview, and exegete their culture. Much of that, you would do in a classroom, but the most important lessons would take place by interacting with the Khosa tribe.

The same is true regarding this book and you. In order to write this book, we actually asked the younger unchurched their views on issues. Sound like a clever idea? Well, we're not that smart. It just seemed that if you want to know about a group of people, you should ask those people. And let me add, you should not just read this book. You should spend some time listening to and talking to unchurched young people.

Our research will point to generalizations and trends, but those tendencies are not people. Unchurched Harry, Ally, Dean, or whoever are fiction. We think they provide helpful contrasts, but they don't really exist. But the lost guy next to you is real. So learn about the trends, and then, go meet your neighbors.

Data regarding the unchurched came from several surveys. The two primary ones[1] included a study of nine hundred young adults from the U.S. and Canada and a study of five hundred older Americans for comparison. We then asked questions several different ways to parse for more information. The process lasted from 2006 to early 2008.

So Who Are They?

While it's always easy (though sometimes not helpful) to start by describing what a "generic" person looks like, it is important to do so in many ways. Also, it adds to the credibility of the conversation when we admit that the next generation is not made up of only young white Americans. (It seems like many conferences on reaching young adults are run by white people with goatees—like me.)

So what do they look like? Well, our sample looks like America—and intentionally so. Racially, the twenty- to twenty-nine-year-old unchurched were 69 percent Anglo (white non-Hispanic), 13 percent Hispanic, 13 percent African-American, and 5 percent other or mixed races. There was about a forty to sixty split between those age twenty to twenty-four and those twenty-five to twenty-nine. Twenty-five percent were married, 67 percent had never been married, 4 percent were in civil unions or domestic partnerships, and 3 percent had been married but were either divorced, widowed, or separated.

Those who talked to us indicated they were more educated than national estimates from the U.S. Census Bureau would have predicted.[2] Over half of the age twenty- to twenty-nine unchurched folks interviewed said they were college graduates. Another 35 percent had attended some college, meaning that eight out of nine pursued post-secondary education.

Based on census estimates, the expectation would have been that about half of the younger unchurched would have matriculated to college at some level. That the unchurched population is more educated than the general population agrees with other findings in the research. In the end, churches that want to reach unchurched twenty- to twenty-nine-year-olds must prepare to address both the educated and the uneducated.

Spiritual but Not Religious

People often tell us today that they are spiritual (with a smile), but that is often followed by (with a frown), "but I am not religious." When asked to describe their own personal religious or spiritual beliefs, 43 percent of the younger unchurched said they were spiritual but not religious. Another 31 percent claimed to be both spiritual and religious. Only 9 percent were religious but not spiritual, and 18 percent said they were neither spiritual nor religious. It is exceedingly inaccurate to think that young adults do not consider themselves to be spiritual. They do, but more consider themselves "spiritual, but not religious," than consider themselves "spiritual and religious." Just a few (and one has to wonder what church would want religious but not spiritual people) label themselves "religious" but not "spiritual."

Obviously this creates some challenges—especially when the younger unchurched value spiritual matters but are turned off by religion. At this point, the situation gets complicated because most of you reading this book are religious. Even if you don't think of yourself as such, the unchurched probably do.

Intriguingly, even though church attendance is not important (this is by definition—in order to be in the sample, they must not attend a church), 40 percent of the young unchurched identify with a denomination or faith group. Only 16 percent said they belong to an organization or club that provides the same experience or feeling they might expect in a church. Asked to choose their religious affiliation, respondents most often chose Protestant or other non-denominational Christian (36 percent) and Roman Catholic (22 percent). Almost 30 percent chose either no religion or named something other than Christian, Jewish (3 percent), and Muslim (1 percent). The other 9 percent claimed to be in the atheist/realist/humanist camp. Furthermore, only 28 percent of the Protestant respondents considered themselves to be born-again, evangelical, or fundamentalist Christians.

Have the younger unchurched always been unchurched? Certainly not. Surprisingly, more than 60 percent reported attending church weekly when they were growing up. As we discussed in chapter one, it may be better to call them the de-churched, than the unchurched. How did churches lose the young generation? And is there any hope for reclaiming the former churched and claiming the never churched? Stay tuned.

Beliefs about God

It seemed a good place to start . . . so we asked what people thought about God. Respondents were read a series of four statements about God and asked for their level of agreement with each statement. Overall responses to these statements are given in Table 1. In the next chapter, we will show how these views compared to the older unchurched—and I think you will find it interesting.

Table 1: Beliefs about God, Age 20–29	20–29	20–24	25–29
God, or a higher supreme being, actually exists.	81%	81%	80%
There exists only one God, the God described in the Bible.	57%	61%	54%
The existence of God does or would have an impact on the way you live your life.	74%	77%	72%
The God of the Bible is no different from the gods or spiritual beings depicted by world religions such as Islam, Hinduism, Buddhism, etc.	58%	56%	59%

God Exists

Four out of five unchurched adults in America between the ages of twenty and twenty-nine believe that a supreme being exists. Like most of the unchurched, the younger unchurched believe in God. This is a foundational beginning point as Christians reach out to them.

God Impacts

Even though they are not attending church, three of four claim that the existence of God does or would impact their lives. It just appears that the impact does not translate into involvement in a church. However, the belief that God's existence should make a difference can certainly present an opportunity to discuss how He can change people's lives.

But Which God?

"God exists" certainly does not imply an understanding of, or faith in, the God of the Bible. Little willingness exists to indicate that God means only the God described in the Bible. It is still a majority, but much less prevalent. That points out two interesting things.

First, the majority of the younger unchurched actually do believe in God and believe that He is the God described in the Bible. Second, a significant number believe in God, but they are not sure the God of the Bible is the only God.

Since 57 percent believe that only the God described in the Bible exists, that is an opportunity to build on that belief and begin conversations about a personal relationship with Jesus Christ. However, 58 percent believe the biblical God is no different from gods or spiritual beings worshipped by other world religions such as Islam, Hinduism, Buddhism, etc. I guess we shouldn't be surprised that people who don't go to church don't understand how completely different the God of the Bible is from Hinduism's pantheon or Buddhism's idea that ultimate reality is impersonal nonexistence.

Furthermore, of those who agree that only the biblical God exists, 53 percent still agree that God is no different from other gods. Put simply, an abundance of spiritual confusion permeates the belief system of the young unchurched. When you add those views to the Oprah-ization of American Christianity, you get a generic "big guy in the sky" view of God and a "you believe what you believe, I believe what I believe" viewpoint on theology. Young people are shocked when Christians say the Bible explains the truth about who God is, what He expects of people, and what He has done to make it possible for us to be reconciled with Him. Shocked, but not closed to discussions.

Ethnicity

Ethnic Americans who are young and unchurched are even stronger in their belief that God exists. Ninety-eight percent of young

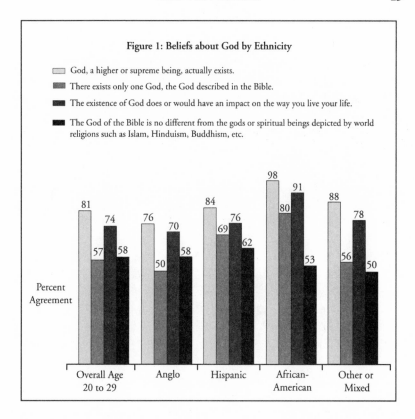

Figure 1: Beliefs about God by Ethnicity

unchurched African-Americans and 84 percent of Hispanics agreed that God exists, compared to 76 percent of unchurched Anglos age twenty to twenty-nine. African-Americans also expressed greater agreement with the existence of only the God of the Bible, 80 percent compared to Hispanics (69 percent) and Anglos (50 percent). African-Americans were the only group that differed (90 percent compared to 72 percent of the others combined) in their agreement that God's existence does or would impact the way they lived. Agreement that the biblical God is similar to the gods of other religions was slightly elevated among Hispanics (61 percent), but this reached the 50 percent level for all ethnicities measured.

Spiritual and Religious

Recall that the younger unchurched are likely to describe themselves as more spiritual than religious. Among the 72 percent that identified themselves as spiritual (combines "Both" and "Spiritual Only" in Figure 2):

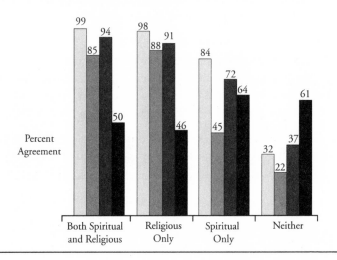

Figure 2: Beliefs about God by Spiritual and Religious

☐ God, a higher or supreme being, actually exists.

■ There exists only one God, the God described in the Bible.

■ The existence of God does or would have an impact on the way you live your life.

■ The God of the Bible is no different from the gods or spiritual beings depicted by world religions such as Islam, Hinduism, Buddhism, etc.

- 90 percent agree that God exists,
- 62 percent agree that only the God of the Bible exists,
- 81 percent agreed that the existence of God does or would have an impact on their lifestyle, and
- 58 percent agree that the God of the Bible is no different than the gods of other religions.

For the sake of comparison, beliefs about God among the 28 percent of those not describing themselves as spiritual, the numbers were:

- 56 percent agree that God exists,
- 45 percent agree that only the God of the Bible exists,
- 56 percent agreed that the existence of God does or would have an impact on their lifestyle, and
- 56 percent agree that the God of the Bible is no different than the gods of other religions.

The area with the most agreement between the spiritual and unspiritual young adults was that the God of the Bible was no different than other gods. Spiritual or unspiritual, the majority agrees in a bland God. But the more spiritual someone is, a higher agreement exists surrounding the biblical God and His impact on lifestyle.

Of those claiming to be spiritual, 42 percent also said they were religious. Those who identified themselves as "spiritual and religious" had views closer to evangelical Christian beliefs. Among the "spiritual and religious" group:

- 99 percent believe that God exists;
- 85 percent agree that only the biblical God exists,
- 94 percent agreed that God's existence impacted their life, yet half agreed that the biblical God is no different from gods of other world religions such as Islam, Hinduism, and Buddhism.

Religious, spiritual, both, or neither, the majority agrees that God, god, or gods all work pretty well and can easily coexist.

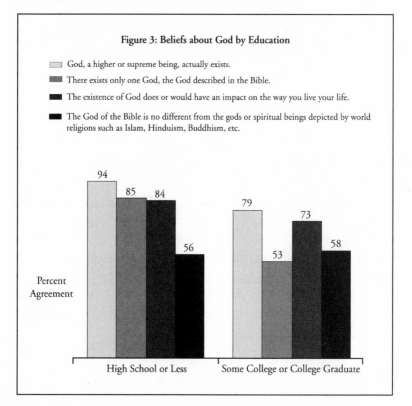

Figure 3: Beliefs about God by Education

God, a higher or supreme being, actually exists.

There exists only one God, the God described in the Bible.

The existence of God does or would have an impact on the way you live your life.

The God of the Bible is no different from the gods or spiritual beings depicted by world religions such as Islam, Hinduism, Buddhism, etc.

Percent Agreement

High School or Less: 94, 85, 84, 56

Some College or College Graduate: 79, 53, 73, 58

Education

The sample of unchurched twenty- to twenty-nine-year-olds was highly educated, which has a strong influence on belief systems. The effect of education can be captured by comparing beliefs of the 88 percent of the young unchurched with at least some college to the 12 percent with high school or less education. Those with college exposure were less likely to believe that God exists, 79 percent compared to 94 percent of those with high school or less education. Agreement that only the God of the Bible exists was only 53 percent among the more educated; it was 85 percent among the less educated unchurched in their twenties. Less education led to a stronger agreement that God's existence affected their life (84 percent versus 73 percent). As the mind is expanded by education, some of the extra space is filled with tolerance of false notions about God.

Prior Church Experience

At least two ways can be used to evaluate the younger unchurched's former connection to church: identification with a denomination or faith group ("I am a Methodist, I just don't go.") and frequency of church attendance as a child ("I used to be a Lutheran."). Two out of five younger unchurched identify with a denomination or faith group, and three out of five reported attending church weekly as a child. Each of these characteristics strengthens agreement about the existence and impact of God.

The unchurched twentysomethings that currently identify with a denomination or faith group were more likely to believe that God exists (93 percent to 73 percent of those without denominational identity), and they were substantially more likely to believe only the God of the Bible exists (72 percent to 47 percent) and to agree that the existence of God does or would impact their life (86 percent to 66 percent).

Those who attended church weekly as a child were more likely to believe that God exists (85 percent to 73 percent of those that attended church less than weekly as a child), to believe that only the God of the Bible exists (64 percent to 46 percent), and to agree that the existence of God does or would impact their life (79 percent to 65 percent).

Identifying with a denomination is a more current indicator of religiosity than childhood church attendance; hence, it is more strongly associated with increased agreement regarding beliefs about God.

Beliefs about Jesus

For Christians, believing in God is one thing. Believing in and properly understanding who Jesus is and what He did is essential. Respondents were asked to reply to two specific statements about Jesus.

Table 2: Beliefs about Jesus, Age 20–29	Agree
Jesus died and came back to life.	66%
Believing in Jesus makes a positive difference in a person's life.	77%

The gospel is all about Jesus. The ultimate questions for all of humanity relate to Him. The unchurched were asked whether they agreed that Jesus died and came back to life and whether believing in Jesus makes a positive difference in a person's life—two things that one would think should be connected.

Obviously, believing that Jesus died and came back to life does not make one a Christian—but you cannot be a Christian without believing that. So, a person who agrees with the basic Christian tenet of the resurrection of Jesus may be more receptive to an opportunity to trust in Jesus. More than 60 percent of persons age twenty to twenty-nine (not in church in the last six months) agreed, either strongly or somewhat, that Jesus died and came back to life. About 30 percent disagreed, and 7 percent answered that they were not sure. Fully, two-thirds of those with an opinion agreed with this statement.

Simply put, the younger unchurched are not staying away from church because they have a problem with Jesus. About three out of four agree that believing in Jesus makes a positive difference in a person's life. That is good news if we are interested in living like Jesus and sharing Jesus with people. Although, it's probably not great news if we are just concerned about getting people to come to church.

I asked my friend Dan Kimball to respond to the data. He has written a helpful book called *They Like Jesus but Not the Church*. Dan shared:

> This data doesn't surprise me. Having directly served in youth and young adult ministry more than eighteen years, I have listened to all types of stories and beliefs and this

matches exactly. That is why I have so much optimism. People are open to the person of Jesus and are interested in Him. I am aware that many do not understand who the biblical Jesus is in regards to His divinity, the atonement, His future return, and judgment. But because they are interested in what they do know about Him—a teacher who went against legalism and "religion" and cared for the poor—that opens the door for having further dialogue about the teachings of Jesus they may not know about. If we listen to what they believe, we'll have a better understanding of what to talk further about with them. I have seen God use this openness to Jesus to bring people into His kingdom. We have baptized many over the years who started with a limited knowledge of Jesus, but then they learned about salvation, the gospel, the cross, about sin and repentance. They eventually made decisions to change and follow the biblical Jesus.

At the same time I express optimism, it also is important to state that we (I should say us being used by the Holy Spirit) have many barriers to overcome. Yes, the data shows people are open to Jesus' resurrection and Him coming back from the dead, but they are also open to reincarnation and karma. Many are open to mixing a few Hindu beliefs with some Buddhism, tossed together with forms of pantheism.

It's great when someone believes in "Jesus" and that He rose from dead, but we need to explore what else he or she may believe. It is very much like being a missionary in another culture. As any missionary studies and seeks to understand the beliefs of the people group they are missionaries to, we need to do this here today.[3]

Ethnicity

In many ways, ethnicity shapes one's beliefs. We found that several of the demographic and other factors that impact beliefs about God also impact beliefs about Jesus. Once again, African-Americans have stronger agreement with both statements about Jesus than any other racial or ethnic group. Almost all African-American young adults (98 percent) agree that Jesus died and came back to life, and eight out of nine agree

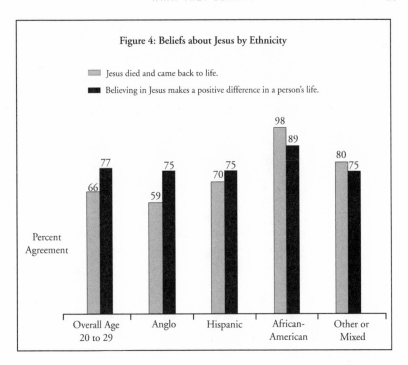

Figure 4: Beliefs about Jesus by Ethnicity

that believing in Jesus makes a positive difference in a person's life. On the other hand, only 59 percent of Anglos believe in the resurrection. Hispanics were similar to the total group, as 70 percent agreed that Jesus returned to life. Agreement that believing in Jesus made a positive difference in a person's life was 75 percent for each of the non-African-American groups.

Spiritual and Religious

Not surprisingly, younger unchurched people in their twenties, who identified themselves as neither spiritual nor religious, hold a comparatively low view of Jesus. Only one-fourth of this group agreed that Jesus died and came back to life, and only half agreed that believing in Jesus had a positive effect on a person. In contrast, those claiming to be both spiritual and religious were 90 percent in agreement with the resurrection and 95 percent in agreement with positive influence of Jesus in the lives of believers.

A larger contrast existed between the religious and nonreligious on both questions about Jesus than between the spiritual and nonspiritual.

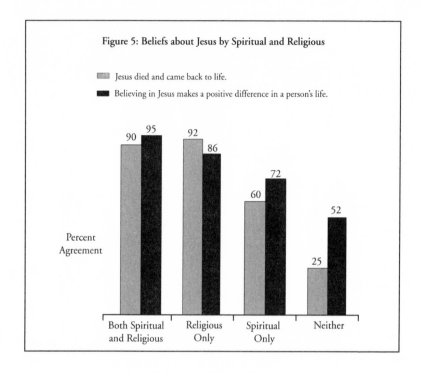

Figure 5: Beliefs about Jesus by Spiritual and Religious

▨ Jesus died and came back to life.

■ Believing in Jesus makes a positive difference in a person's life.

Education

Similar to the beliefs about God, agreement with both statements about Jesus declines when a young unchurched person has college experience. Belief in the resurrection drops from 92 percent among the less educated (high school or less) to 63 percent among those with some college or a degree. The similar contrast is less drastic (90 percent versus 75 percent) when considering agreement that believing in Jesus makes a positive difference.

Prior Church Experience

If you attended church as a child, it impacts your beliefs later. Church attendance as a child and current denominational or faith group identity both have positive effects on beliefs about Jesus.

The unchurched twentysomethings that currently identify with a denomination or faith group were more likely to agree that Jesus died and was resurrected (77 percent compared to 59 percent of those without current denominational identity), and to agree that believing

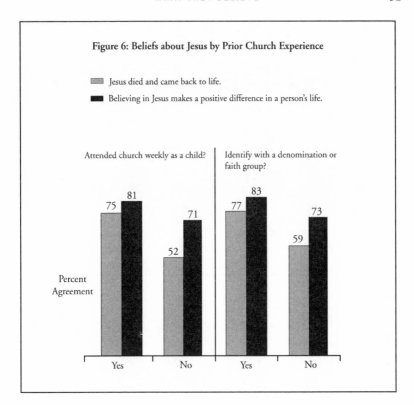

Figure 6: Beliefs about Jesus by Prior Church Experience

■ Jesus died and came back to life.

■ Believing in Jesus makes a positive difference in a person's life.

in Jesus makes a positive difference in a person's life (83 percent to 73 percent).

Those who attended church weekly as a child were more likely to believe the Easter story (75 percent to 52 percent of those that attended church less than weekly as a child), and to agree that the belief in Jesus is a positive influence on people (81 percent to 71 percent).

When we look at the younger unchurched, the de-churched (those who once attended but now do not) do tend to think and believe differently than those who have little or no church experience . . . and that impacts how people are reached.

Beliefs about the Christian Church

When you start talking about the local church, opinions vary. In the case of the younger unchurched, they have some strong opinions on the subject. Questions aimed at perceptions of the Christian church uncovered real angst about organized religion among the young unchurched.

Table 3: Beliefs about the Christian Church	Agree
The Christian church is generally helpful to society as a whole.	73%
I do not think my lifestyle would be accepted at most Christian churches.	39%
The church is full of hypocrites, people who criticize others for doing the same thing they do themselves.	67%
I believe I can have a good relationship with God without being involved in a church.	90%
The church is the only place to learn what it means to be a Christian.	9%

Nearly three quarters expressed at least some level of agreement that the Christian church is generally helpful to society as a whole. This was by far the most favorable response to the church by those in their twenties who do not attend. The younger unchurched believe that the church can make a positive difference.

However, the church does not create warm fuzzy feelings among Americans outside her fold. Among the younger unchurched, two out of three agree that the church is full of hypocrites, people who criticize others for doing the same things they are doing themselves. An overwhelming sense that the church is filled with hypocrites emanates from the younger unchurched.

For some, their lifestyle may be a concern that lowers their interest in church. Thirty-nine percent do not believe their current lifestyle would be accepted at church—which tends to be a problem if the intent is to reach them.

Yet, many of the younger unchurched may be unconcerned about their church involvement—about nine out of ten believe they do not need the church in order to have a good relationship with God or to learn what it means to be a Christian.

It is interesting to compare the differences of the unchurched under twenties and the unchurched over thirty. As might be expected due to lifestyle issues, unchurched Americans in their twenties are more concerned that their lifestyles would not be acceptable at church (39 percent to 30 percent) and less concerned about hypocrites in the church (67 percent to 75 percent) than the thirty and over group. We will more closely compare these two age groups in chapter 3.

African-Americans

Unchurched African-American respondents age twenty to twenty-nine differ from their peers as to their views of church. Eight of nine (89 percent) agree that the church is generally useful to society, compared to seven out of ten Anglos and 78 percent of Hispanics. Young unchurched African-Americans also agree more than others (25 percent to 7 percent) that the church is the only place to learn what it means to be a Christian.

Since African-Americans hold higher opinions about God, Jesus, and the church, why are they not attending church? One reason may be that they are more concerned about hypocrites in the church and are more likely than other races to agree that their lifestyle would not be accepted at most Christian churches. Should African-American churches and Christians take hope in the beliefs of their young people?

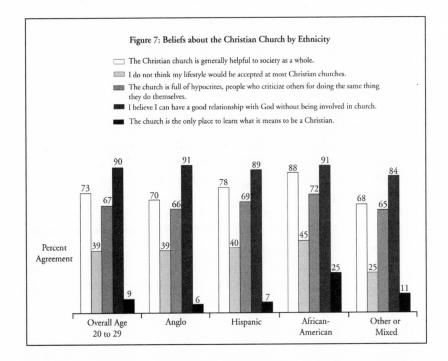

Figure 7: Beliefs about the Christian Church by Ethnicity

☐ The Christian church is generally helpful to society as a whole.

▨ I do not think my lifestyle would be accepted at most Christian churches.

▩ The church is full of hypocrites, people who criticize others for doing the same thing they do themselves.

■ I believe I can have a good relationship with God without being involved in church.

■ The church is the only place to learn what it means to be a Christian.

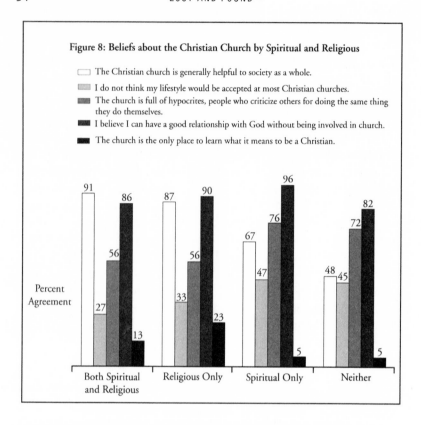

Figure 8: Beliefs about the Christian Church by Spiritual and Religious

☐ The Christian church is generally helpful to society as a whole.

▨ I do not think my lifestyle would be accepted at most Christian churches.

■ The church is full of hypocrites, people who criticize others for doing the same thing they do themselves.

▨ I believe I can have a good relationship with God without being involved in church.

■ The church is the only place to learn what it means to be a Christian.

Yes. Should they be concerned that those beliefs are not being incorporated into lifestyles that the church would accept? Absolutely.

Spiritual and Religious

Self-identification as spiritual and or religious has predictable influence on beliefs about the church. The younger unchurched who are "religious" are more likely to agree that the church is generally helpful to society (90 percent compared to 63 percent). Fewer have concerns that their own lifestyle would be frowned upon at church (28 percent to 46 percent), yet 85 percent still think you can learn to be a Christian somewhere other than church.

Whether a young adult is spiritual has little impact on his or her view of the church, since spirituality is not derived from nor related directly to the organized church.

Education

The views of the younger unchurched differ greatly based on education. Concerning their beliefs about the church, differences are most prevalent between the least educated (less than high school) and the other groups. The least educated group was a small proportion of the sample and caution must be used in separating their responses for analysis. However, it is interesting to note that 80 percent of the least educated younger unchurched felt their lifestyle would be unacceptable at most churches. This is the same group with the highest opinion of the church—80 percent agree with the general helpfulness of the church and only 49 percent view the church as full of hypocrites. The question lingers for the least educated as it does for African-Americans—*Why are there lifestyle issues among this group with a high view of the church?*

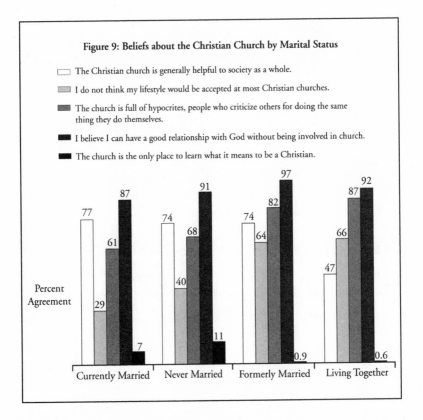

Figure 9: Beliefs about the Christian Church by Marital Status

☐ The Christian church is generally helpful to society as a whole.

▨ I do not think my lifestyle would be accepted at most Christian churches.

▦ The church is full of hypocrites, people who criticize others for doing the same thing they do themselves.

■ I believe I can have a good relationship with God without being involved in church.

■ The church is the only place to learn what it means to be a Christian.

Marital Status

Views tend to change depending upon relationship status. The younger unchurched who are currently married and never married have higher positive views of the church than the formerly married and those currently in civil or domestic relationships (living together). Less than half of those in a civil or domestic relationship agree that the church is generally helpful to society.

Two out of three formerly married persons and those in a civil or domestic relationship feel their current lifestyle would not be accepted at most Christian churches. (The comparable proportion of married respondents was 30 percent.) Over 80 percent of formerly married persons and those in a civil or domestic relationship agree the church is full of hypocrites, and almost 100 percent of each group agree you can learn what it means to be Christian outside of church. Four percent of the younger unchurched are living together, 3 percent are formerly married, widowed, or divorced, and their receptivity to the church is greatly diminished.

Open to People but Not to the Church

It would not be an understatement to say the unchurched dislike the church. In many ways, that is self-evident. They are, after all, the UN-churched. In a context where churches exist, they have rejected them.

However, we were surprised at just how open the younger unchurched actually are to hearing about Christianity. In overwhelming percentages, the younger unchurched expressed an openness in regard to hearing their friends talk about Christ.

They may not be open to an invitation to church, but they certainly are open to an invitation to conversation:

Table 4: What Can Individual Christians Do?	Agree
If someone wanted to tell me what she or he believed about Christianity, I would be willing to listen.	89%
I would be willing to study the Bible if a friend asked me to.	61%
If a friend told you he or she recently became a Christian, this would have a positive effect on your relationship.	47%

Some interesting and surprising numbers surface here—and a great opportunity. Almost 90 percent of the unchurched twenty- to twenty-nine-year-olds said they would be willing to listen if someone wanted to tell them about Christianity.

The stakes are raised when a friend talks to an unchurched person. Three out of five younger unchurched respondents agreed they would be willing to study the Bible if a friend asked them to do so.

The Christian conversion of a friend may directly impact an unchurched person. Just under half of the unchurched in their twenties agreed that a friend becoming a Christian would have a positive effect on their relationship.

Subgroups

Practically every subgroup of the young unchurched population is willing to listen if someone wanted to tell them what he or she believes about Christianity. Young adults living together in a civil union or domestic relationship are slightly less willing to listen (73 percent), as are persons of other or mixed races (77 percent). Although the sample is smaller here, the numbers are still helpful.

If invited by a friend to study the Bible, 86 percent of the least educated respondents would be willing. Other subgroups with more receptivity than the overall 61 percent included those identifying themselves as religious (74 percent), those who said they were Protestant by religion (78 percent), and African-Americans (73 percent). Groups less agreeable to studying the Bible with a friend include those in civil or domestic partner relationships (42 percent) and Hispanics (50 percent).

Interestingly, two-thirds of religious respondents said a friend's conversion to Christianity would improve their relationship compared to one-third of the nonreligious. Less education was associated with a higher agreement that a friend's conversion would have a positive impact.

Young unchurched folks with prior and current religious experience were more likely to receive a friend's conversion as good news. Over half of those who attended church weekly as a child, and 57 percent of those who currently identify with a denomination or faith group, agreed that a friend's conversion to Christianity would improve their relationship with their friend.

African-Americans were more likely (70 percent) and Hispanics were less likely (38 percent) to view a friend's conversion as a positive for their relationship.

How Do Churches Reach the Unchurched?

We will share later how churches are effectively reaching young adults. Before we get to that, it is significant to note that the survey also reveals further responses related specifically to churches. Contrary to what some might think, a great worship band is not (always and only) the answer. Understandability and caring rise above other factors. Willingness to join a small group is a strong minority consideration. Yet, less than a third indicate that it is the music's familiarity that would make them more likely to attend.

Table 5: What Can Churches Do?	Agree
If a church presented truth to me in an understandable way that relates to my life now, I would attend.	63%
If people at church cared about me as a person, I would be more likely to attend.	58%
I would be willing to join a small group of people to learn more about the Bible and Jesus.	46%
If music at church sounded similar to my favorite type of music, I would be more likely to attend.	31%

The survey included questions aimed at determining what churches might do to encourage an unchurched person in his or her twenties to attend. The statement in this category garnering most agreement related to presenting truth in an understandable way that relates to the respondent's life now. More than 60 percent said they would attend church if this happened. (Suggestion number one—do this!) And while presenting truth in an understandable and relevant way, we might also want to try caring about the unchurched as individuals. Almost 60 percent said this would encourage them to attend.

As an outreach activity, starting small groups certainly seems to provide an opportunity. Almost half of the younger unchurched agreed they would be willing to join such a group. Based on the previous responses, an invitation from a friend to attend such a small group may be the entry point for proving to the unchurched that Christians care about them.

Ethnicity

African-Americans again showed the most agreement to this set of questions. Eighty-four percent agreed they would attend if a church presented truth to them in an understandable way that relates to their life now, 69 percent would be willing to join a small group to learn about the Bible and Jesus, 76 percent would be influenced to attend a church that cared about them, and 50 percent would be influenced by the choice of music.

Hispanics would respond to a lesser extent to the same stimuli as African-Americans, while these factors have less impact on Anglos and persons of other or mixed races.

Spiritual and Religious

We wrote earlier that 74 percent of the young unchurched described themselves as spiritual. Though not as open to these four outreach ideas as those identifying themselves as religious, the spiritual majority is more responsive than their peers who are not spiritual.

Sixty-nine percent of spiritual young unchurched folks (compared to 49 percent not spiritual) agreed they would attend if a church presented truth to them in an understandable way that relates to their life now. Fifty percent would be willing to join a small group to learn about the Bible and Jesus, 63 percent would be influenced to attend by a church that cared about them, and 34 percent would be influenced by the choice of music.

Self-described religious persons in there twenties would also respond strongly to the same ideas, but their numbers are not as large as those who are spiritual.

Education

Attending and graduating from college seems to desensitize the younger unchurched to matters of religion. Sixty-two percent of those exposed to college agreed they would attend a church that presented truth to them in an understandable way that related to their life now, compared to 72 percent of those who never attended college. The less educated respondents were more sensitive to churches that care about them and use music styles to which they relate. Eighty-two percent of respondents with less than a high school education would be willing to join a small group to learn about the Bible and Jesus, compared to 39 percent of college graduates.

Prior Church Experience

The unchurched population in their twenties are more responsive to each of these four measures of church outreach if they attended church weekly as a child and if they currently identify with a denomination or faith group.

Marital Status

Young adults currently married or never married held similar views as the overall group in their responses to church efforts to reach them. Divorced, separated, or widowed adults in their twenties would respond to a larger degree (74 percent) to understandable truths and to churches that cared about them as persons (71 percent). None of these ideas for churches would encourage young adults living together to attend.

A Deeper Look at Spirituality

When an unchurched person responds that they are spiritual, what does that mean? When asked about their level of agreement with the statement, "I consider myself to be spiritual because I am interested in knowing more about God, or a higher supreme being," 73 percent of the unchurched in their twenties registered either strong or somewhat agreement.

Table 6: A Deeper Look at Spirituality	Agree
I consider myself to be spiritual because I am interested in knowing more about God, or a higher supreme being.	73%
Most of my friends are spiritual.	54%
People who attend a Christian church are generally more spiritual than those who do not attend.	39%

This spirituality is widespread. Five out of nine respondents agreed that most of their friends are spiritual. Because this question immediately followed the question that provided a definition, it should be safe to assume the friends are also considered spiritual because they are interested in knowing more about God, or a higher supreme being. On the other hand, unchurched twentysomethings are not convinced that attending a Christian church indicates an increased spirituality—only a minority indicated that those who attend are more spiritual.

The younger unchurched are clearly making a distinction between spirituality and religion. For them, being spiritual or having curiosity about God is more important than attending church. After all, they also told us they do not need a church in order to learn what it means to be a Christian, nor to have a good relationship with God.

Subgroups

Several groups within the younger unchurched population are even more intense about their spirituality. For example, 95 percent of those who identified themselves earlier as both spiritual and religious agreed with the follow-up question containing the definition of spirituality. Other groups with elevated curiosity about God included those that identified with a denomination or faith group (81 percent), especially Protestants (87 percent), as well as African-Americans (91 percent), Hispanics (82 percent), and those with high school or less education (88 percent).

Considering the question about the spirituality of their friends, two interesting groups were divided in their response. Forty-eight percent of unchurched respondents age twenty to twenty-four expressed agreement that most of their friends were spiritual, compared to 58 percent of those age twenty-five to twenty-nine. The data rarely distinguishes between the younger twenties and the older twenties.

Similarly, few distinctions are evident between male and female respondents. In this case, however, 61 percent of females and 48 percent of males agreed that most of their friends are spiritual.

Heaven? and Hell?

Lots of evangelicals like the question, "If you were to die today, do you know if you would go to heaven or hell?" Well, for the majority of younger unchurched, their eternal destination is not often on their minds. The survey asked, "How often do you wonder, 'If I were to die today, would I go to heaven?'" The distribution of responses among the twenty- to twenty-nine-year-olds was: 9 percent daily, 15 percent weekly, 22 percent monthly, 15 percent yearly, and 40 percent never or not sure. Fifty-nine percent of the unchurched population age thirty and over said they never wondered about their eternal destiny.

Eventually, an evangelistic witness to an unchurched person must deal with issues of eternity, but that may not be the best place to start. Since only 45 percent wonder about their eternal destination more than once a year, what are their beliefs about eternity?

Table 7: Heaven and Hell	Agree
When a person dies, his or her spirit continues to exist in an afterlife.	82%
There exists a place of reward in the afterlife, sometimes called heaven.	77%
There exists a place of punishment in the afterlife, sometimes called hell.	60%
My belief about the existence of an afterlife has an impact on the way I live.	63%

More than four out of five younger unchurched respondents agree that when a person dies, his or her spirit continues to live in an afterlife, a view held by all major faith groups. Majority beliefs include the existence of places of reward (77 percent) and punishment (60 percent) in the afterlife. The de-emphasis of hell from mainline and even evangelical pulpits has impacted the younger unchurched generation. Additionally, 63 percent agree that their beliefs about the afterlife impact the way they live.

Among those who wonder at least monthly if they would go to heaven, agreement with all of the other questions about an afterlife is amplified. Over 90 percent of those who wonder about their eternal destination agree that the spirit continues and that heaven exists. About 80 percent agree that hell exists and that their belief about the afterlife affects their lifestyle. So, the "How often do you wonder" question may not be the best icebreaker to use with an unchurched person, but it does reveal a lot about his or her beliefs about the afterlife.

Segments of the young unchurched population that indicated higher agreement with the afterlife questions included those who described themselves as spiritual and/or religious, those with a denominational or faith group identity, those with lower educational levels, African-Americans, and females.

Christianity

Although the younger unchurched agree that Christianity is a relevant and viable religion, they were harsh in their judgment that Christianity is more about organized religion than loving God and people. The younger unchurched think the churched are not living the faith they espouse.

Table 8: Christianity	Agree
The Christian religion is a relevant and viable religion for today.	74%
I think Christianity today is more about organized religion than about loving God and loving people.	77%

The unchurched in their twenties who described themselves as both spiritual and religious (91 percent), those who identified with a denomination or faith group (84 percent), those who never attended college (87 percent), and those mixed or other race (91 percent) all agreed in large proportions that Christianity is relevant and viable as a religion.

Younger unchurched respondents who are formerly married (93 percent) and those in civil or domestic relationships (94 percent) expressed high agreement that Christianity is more about organized religion rather than loving God and people. This and other indicators point to the lack of acceptance by Christian churches felt particularly by divorced, widowed, and separated young people.

Searching for Guidance

A person seeking inspirational or spiritual guidance in today's culture has a plethora of choices. Survey participants were asked for one source they would consult.

"Which of the following sources would you consult if you were seeking inspirational guidance?"

- 41 percent would talk or listen to an inspirational person
- 22 percent would read an inspirational book
- 17 percent would go to church
- 8 percent would watch an inspirational movie

- 7 percent would search the Internet
- 5 percent were not sure what they would do

The survey also asked specifically about television and the Internet as sources of spiritual guidance. Agreement levels with these two statements are given in Table 9.

Table 9: Spiritual Guidance	Agree
I have searched for spiritual help online.	37%
Sometimes I watch a Christian television program.	19%

While searching for inspirational guidance, the younger unchurched turn primarily to a person whom they think is inspirational. The person may be a local minister, but it may also be Oprah Winfrey or another "inspirational" celebrity. The younger unchurched told us clearly that they would respond best to personal attention from a caring church or small group.

More would prefer to read an inspirational book (maybe the Bible) rather than seek inspirational help from a church. *Remarkably, only one in six would go to church if seeking spiritual guidance.* This should give church leaders reason to pause and examine its availability and presentation to the twenty- to twenty-nine-year-olds not in church.

Even though only 7 percent listed the Internet as the primary source of guidance, 37 percent have searched for spiritual help online.

Christian television is watched sometimes by 19 percent of the younger unchurched. Viewership is much stronger among African-Americans (57 percent), formerly married young people (59 percent), less educated (83 percent with less than high school), and those with Protestant identity (52 percent).

Relating to Christians

In a pluralistic society, unchurched persons encounter Christians regularly. In fact, they say that some of their best friends are Christians! So what do young people outside of church think of Christians?

Table 10: Relationships with Christians	Agree
I have at least one close friend who considers himself or herself a Christian.	91%
I have many Christian friends.	69%
Christians get on my nerves.	46%

Nine out of ten young adults not in church have at least one Christian among their close friends. This does not imply that the Christian friend is churched. What if the Christians invited their unchurched friends to study the Bible? Voila! Sixty percent already said they would do so. Ninety percent would listen to someone tell them what they believed about Christianity, and 46 percent would be willing to join a small group to learn about the Bible and Jesus.

One of the more interesting questions that we asked was to agree or disagree with the statement, "Christians get on my nerves." We released this and a couple of other questions from the study, and this one was picked up by USA Today and CNN.

I had an interesting conversation with the CNN anchor about this question. We discussed the research and focused on the reputation of Christians and how surprisingly negative people were toward Christians—even to the point of saying that they were hypocrites and Christians get on their nerves.

It is hard to imagine that 46 percent of respondents would be willing to say that Jews or Muslims get on their nerves. Simply put, we have a reputation problem.

Every segment of the unchurched population has substantial Christian friends and acquaintances (however they define Christian in their own mind). Only Jews (79 percent) and Muslims (60 percent) reported less than 80 percent agreement when asked if they had at least one close friend that is a Christian. Even 90 percent of those who categorized themselves as atheist, humanist, or realist had a Christian friend.

Although African-Americans are more likely than others to be spiritual and have spiritual friends, they expressed less agreement regarding having close friends (76 percent) and acquaintances (58 percent) that are Christian. Yet, Christians get on their nerves less (32 percent agreement).

In general, having Christian friends did not impact whether Christians get on their nerves. Those registering the most agreement that Christians irritate them include the formerly married (55 percent), those in civil or domestic relationships (69 percent), and the atheist/humanist/realist subgroup (77 percent). Males agree more that Christians get on their nerves than females, 51 percent to 40 percent.

Where Now?

Statistics are tools—but that is all they are. They give us a picture of a generation that is spiritual but wary, open to Jesus but not the church. Yet, this is not all we have to learn about our young unchurched friends. In the next chapter, we will look at the trends of the younger unchurched compared to those who are a bit older.

— A LOST AND FOUND STORY CONTINUED —

Ally Garza shot another glance at her watch and mumbled profanity. "Late again," she chided herself. This time she was determined not to be late. But she was; about thirty minutes. She reached over and rummaged through her duffle-bag-sized purse and found her phone. She slid the keyboard open and started texting with both hands while working the steering wheel of her '88 diesel BMW with her knee.

"B thr n 10," she typed, knowing Dean would already be standing at the curb in front of his apartment. Fortunately it was only about a ten-minute drive from there to the Cozy Note. The thing she hated though is that she'd left him standing in the cold December night air. Then again, given her history, he may have waited before coming down.

She cursed again, this time at her car, as it slowly pulled away from the stoplight. She hated this thing. Not only was it a clunker, it was an environmental disgrace. How could someone whose life was directed toward improving the lives of the less fortunate and saving the environment from greenhouse gasses drive such a vehicle, she thought with disdain. Her car, almost as if to mock her, belched black smoke into the air as she accelerated. She never would have bought it, but after serving two years in Ethiopia with the Peace Corps, she was fortunate to scrape together enough money to buy anything. She'd found it at the back of a lot and bought it from an auto broker who ran his business out of a dilapidated cracker-box house. The red car had been sitting for nine months and was covered in dust.

She was going hybrid all the way, as soon as she could save up the money. Her goal: Toyota Prius. She loved her job with the state human services division, dealing mostly with the homeless and hungry, but the pay was pretty lame. She knew social workers didn't get paid much, but $35,000 a year barely covered rent on her dumpy apartment and fuel for her ragged car.

She was still cursing her car when she whipped to the curb.

"Don't say it, don't even start with me," she fired at Dean before he could even get the door fully open. "I already know I'm going to hear it from Mitch the first chance he gets. I'd bet money he'll even shoot a glance at his watch when he sees us walk in. He'll bring up every time transgression I've ever committed."

Ally's mind drifted back to the first time she and Mitch met. He was a college junior and she was a sophomore. She was late to a required statistics class, and the only open seat was on the front row, next to Mitch. He'd gotten there fifteen minutes early to score a front-row seat. A week into the class, Ally knew she was in trouble. She managed a grade of 43 on the first quiz—panic settled in as she stared blankly at the big, red numbers.

"Good thing we get to drop two quiz scores," she heard a voice say. She turned to see Mitch leaning over to zip his backpack. "I'll bet you do better the next time."

Is he mocking me? she thought, but decided it didn't sound like it. "What'd you make?"

"Ninety-seven," he said, slightly embarrassed.

"How?" she asked with amazement.

"Well, I'm sort of a math geek," he said. "Always have been. Just seems to come kind of natural. I actually like math. Yeah, I know that's weird."

"My head's spinning over here," Ally said. "Like seriously, I studied my butt off for this. If I can't break 50 on the first quiz, how am I going to pass this class which I need to graduate."

"Get a tutor," Mitch suggested with a shrug. "You can arrange it through student services. They're like a couple hundred bucks a semester."

"No way can I afford that!" she gasped. "I'm barely making it as it is. I'm cramming in as many hours as I can at the Starbucks across from campus, but at best I'm getting like twelve hours a week. I can't take a second job right now because I volunteer at the shelter for battered women. I can't give that up."

"I'll do it," he said after a slight pause.

"Do what?"

"Tutor you. I swing by there and get coffee all the time. I could just change my coffee schedule and grab it when you get off. We could spend some time with stats."

"I just told you I can't afford a tutor," she said.

"I heard you, and I'm offering to do it for free," he said, and with a slight grin leaned in and whispered out of the side of his mouth, *"but I won't turn down a contraband cup of coffee every now and then."*

"Why?" she asked in disbelief.

Remembering that moment, as she sputtered into the Cozy Note's parking lot, brought a smile to Ally's face. She still couldn't figure out why Mitch did it, why they continued to be friends after that class ended, and why they were still friends three years after graduation.

It didn't take long for her to learn Mitch was a Christian. She almost dumped him as her tutor when he told her that. At best she'd always been ambivalent toward Christians, but most of the time she was suspicious and critical. They were hypocrites in her mind. She'd determined there was a significant disconnect between what they said and what they did. If they were so loving, how come she never met any down at the women's shelter, or anywhere else there seemed to be a significant need?

Ally also recalled how quickly her former friend Ann's attitude toward her changed after Ann became a Christian. Ally had gotten pregnant during their freshman year and opted for an abortion. Ann went through the roof! Just two months earlier Ann would have driven her to the clinic, now Ann was condemning her for *"taking the life of a baby."* *"What about my life?"* Ally remembered saying to Ann. *"What about what I want? It's my body, and I'll do what I want."*

That was the last time she and Ann had spoken. Ally still shakes her head at the memory. It's one reason she has little to do with religion of any flavor. *"Sure, I've made some mistakes, but overall I think I'm pretty good,"* Ally decided. *"Religion just makes people feel bad."*

The memory of Ann lingered in her mind as she walked through the door and saw Aaron totally into his solo. He sounded great. She and Dean checked their coats and walked toward the table near the front. Sure enough, as soon as they slipped into the light spilling over from the stage Mitch quickly glanced at his watch. Ally waved and coyly shrugged her shoulders. Behind her Dean pointed to Ally and mouthed, *"It was her."* The two of them shook their heads, and Dean saw Mitch chuckle.

Just like Mitch to let it slide, thought Dean. It's hard to believe he's a Christian. He seems so real. I believe he does love me.

What Does the Future Hold?

WHEN OBSERVING THIS YOUNGER GENERATION, IT IS EASY TO say, "They are cynical, arrogant, jaded, or just disinterested." And those statements may well be true in some cases. However, casual evaluations can have their limitations. That's why deliberate research is so important; it reveals specific insights that can make a big difference. For example, if a certain percentage of the younger unchurched have given up on church, that would be good to know. And how does that relate to the generations that came before them? To find out, well . . . again . . . we asked.

Unchurched people in America come in all shapes (physically and spiritually), colors, and ages. While the primary focus of this book is reaching the lost twenty- to twenty-nine-year-olds, it is interesting to compare the younger unchurched with unchurched Americans age thirty and over. Here's a glimpse of those findings. **Younger folks are generally less "fed-up" with religion than older unchurched people.**

Now, we cannot tell if they will get more fed-up as they age or if this is a sign of openness for the future. It is probably some of both. However, in the midst of all the bemoaning about the younger unchurched, we also need to know that they may be more open than their older unchurched counterparts.

As difficult as it may seem to reach the twentysomethings, we have no reason to think they will mellow in their attitudes toward the church as they age. Yet, we do have reason to think they are not as cynical as those who preceded them.

How Do These Two Age Groups Differ?

Some minor demographic differences exist between the samples, but our focus was on their spiritual views. More than 70 percent of the older unchurched seemed turned off by religion compared to 60 percent of the younger set. The Christian church must take advantage of the curiosity of youth, especially as it relates to understanding God or a supreme being. As the unchurched age and have more life experiences, their interest in organized religion diminishes.

Respondents from both age groups have cast their vote against the church by not attending. Yet a sizeable minority of both age groups (40 percent of younger and 30 percent of older unchurched) identify with a denomination or faith group. In other words, though they do not go to church, they still identify themselves, for example, as "Methodists." The younger unchurched are not as jaded toward denominations and religion as the older unchurched, but both groups present significant challenges to churches wishing to reach them.

Are older respondents more turned off by the church because they attended less as children? No, just the opposite seems true. More than 70 percent of the unchurched age thirty and over reported that they attended church weekly as a child compared to 60 percent of the younger group. Exposure as a child was not a positive enough experience to encourage attendance as an adult. For many, they probably had negative experiences. Churches today must realize the responsibility God has given them to provide sound training and positive experiences for children in their care. Poor attitudes toward the church that are established as children may be insurmountable, even with the natural curiosity about spirituality.

Beliefs about God

Revisiting the sets of questions from both surveys allows a deeper comparison between the two groups. Table 1 shows that beliefs about God deteriorate from the younger to the older generations.

Table 1: Beliefs about God[1]	20–29	30+
God, a higher or supreme being, actually exists.	81%	73%
There exists only one God, the God described in the Bible.	57%	48%
The existence of God does or would have an impact on the way I live my life.	74%	68%
The God of the Bible is no different from the gods or spiritual beings depicted by world religions such as Islam, Hinduism, Buddhism, etc.	58%	67%

From a Christian perspective, the younger unchurched answered more correctly in all the categories. They believe in God to a higher degree, they believe in the God of the Bible to a higher degree, they believe that God's existence should impact how they live to a higher degree, and they are more inclined to believe that God is unique in some way from other gods.

If people are open to the gospel, it starts with right beliefs about God. The younger unchurched who participated in this study were more likely than the older unchurched to agree with beliefs about God shared by Christians.

The fact that the unchurched in their twenties have healthier views about God than those age thirty and older does not change the fact that both groups have bad theology. The relatively small numbers who agree that the God described in the Bible is unique in existence and character from those described by other world religions is alarming. How does the evangelical Christian church reach out to the tolerant unchurched with a message of the uniqueness of the true God?

Ethnicity

Beliefs about God across ethnic groups are similar between the two groups surveyed. Looking at both age and ethnicity, the group with the weakest agreement with traditional beliefs about God is unchurched Anglos age thirty and older. Only two in three agree that God exists, with 40 percent agreeing that the God described in the Bible is the only one that exists. Sixty-five percent of older Anglos who are not in church see no distinction between the biblical God and the gods of other world religions.

An overwhelming majority (98 percent) of young unchurched African-Americans and 84 percent of Hispanics agreed that God exists. The strongest agreement that God was no different than others, 84 percent, was held by older Hispanics.

Spiritual and Religious

Among the 68 percent of older unchurched respondents that are spiritual, 85 percent agree that God exists, 56 percent agree that only the God of the Bible exists, 79 percent agree that the existence of God does or would have an impact on their lifestyle, and 66 percent agree that the God of the Bible is no different than the gods of other religions. Comparable levels of agreement among the younger unchurched who described themselves as spiritual were 90 percent, 62 percent, 81 percent, and 58 percent respectively.

Only 36 percent of the older unchurched claiming to be spiritual also said they were religious. Being religious implied stronger agreement with beliefs about God. Of the 30 percent that described themselves as religious, 97 percent believed that God exists; 90 percent agreed that only the biblical God exists; 93 percent agreed that God's existence impacted their life, yet 63 percent agreed that the biblical God is no different from gods of other world religions such as Islam, Hinduism, and Buddhism. These beliefs were similar to the younger unchurched.

Education

The unchurched age thirty and older who went to college have dubious beliefs about God. Only 67 percent of this subset believes that God exists, compared to 93 percent of their age group peers who never attended college. A remarkably low 38 percent agree that only the biblical God exists, and two-thirds of them make no distinction from God and the supreme beings of other religions. Three out of five still claim that the existence of God either does or would have an impact on how they live their lives.

Prior Church Experience

Those who identify with a particular denomination (i.e., "I'm Presbyterian") tend to have more Christian views of God. Those who attended as a child were also impacted positively in their views.

Two indicators of prior church experience are identification with a denomination or faith group and frequency of church attendance as a child. The younger unchurched are more likely to identify with a denomination (40 percent) but less likely to have attended church weekly as a child (60 percent). With the older unchurched, three out of ten identify with a denomination or faith group, and seven out of ten reported attending church weekly as a child. Each of these characteristics strengthens agreement about the existence and impact of God, just as it does among the younger group.

The unchurched over thirty who currently identify with a denomination or faith group were more likely to believe God exists (93 percent compared to 73 percent of those without denominational identity), to believe only the God of the Bible exists (72 percent to 47 percent), and to agree that the existence of God does or would impact their life (86 percent to 66 percent).

Those who attended church weekly as a child were more likely to believe that God exists (76 percent compared to 69 percent of those that attended church less than weekly as a child), to believe that only the God of the Bible exists (50 percent to 44 percent), and to agree that the existence of God does or would impact their life (70 percent to 62 percent).

Identifying with a denomination is a more current indicator of religiosity than childhood church attendance, and it is more strongly associated with increased agreement regarding beliefs about God.

Beliefs about Jesus

Although the focus of this book is the younger unchurched, many of the more alarming responses are from those in the older age group. Table 2 shows that 54 percent of the older group agree strongly or somewhat that Jesus died and came back to life.

Table 2: Beliefs about Jesus	20–29	30+
Jesus died and came back to life.	66%	54%
Believing in Jesus makes a positive difference in a person's life.	77%	73%

The younger unchurched are once again more likely to hold the Christian view. The comparison of the two age groups begs for a witness to the younger unchurched because their beliefs appear to leave them more receptive to the gospel. Both age groups similarly agree that believing in Jesus makes a positive difference in a person's life.

Beliefs about the Christian Church

As best we can tell, the younger unchurched are *not* more upset at the church than the older unchurched. The disconnect between the Christian church and those who do not attend is similar among respondents from both age groups. Table 3 shows that the older respondents were slightly less concerned that their lifestyle would not be accepted at church and more concerned that the church is full of hypocrites. Both of these differences were marginally significant from a statistical perspective, but they may be considerably significant in the church's response to the unchurched.

The most important finding is that neither age group sees a need for the church in regard to having a good relationship with God or learning what it means to be a Christian.

Table 3: Beliefs about the Christian Church	20–29	30+
The Christian church is generally helpful to society as a whole.	73%	72%
I do not think my lifestyle would be accepted at most Christian churches.	39%	30%
The church is full of hypocrites, people who criticize others for doing the same thing they do themselves.	67%	75%
I believe I can have a good relationship with God without being involved in a church.	90%	88%
The church is the only place to learn what it means to be a Christian.	9%	6%

So, yes, the younger unchurched do have a negative view of the church, but it does not seem particularly worse than the older unchurched. In some cases, it is better.

How to Tell?

One of the more remarkable aspects of our study is perhaps one of the most surprising. While many have told of the resistance of the younger unchurched, the loss of faith, and the close-mindedness about Christianity, we found the opposite. **The younger unchurched are more open to hearing about Christ, not less.** A great difference surfaces between the two generations studied in how the unchurched would respond to an appeal from an acquaintance or friend. The minds and hearts of the twenty- to twenty-nine-year-olds seem much more open. Each difference in Table 4 is statistically significant.

Table 4: What Can Individual Christians Do?	20–29	30+
If someone wanted to tell me what she or he believed about Christianity, I would be willing to listen.	89%	75%
I would be willing to study the Bible if a friend asked me to.	61%	42%
If a friend told me he or she recently became a Christian, this would have a positive effect on my relationship.	47%	36%

Both age groups would be willing to listen if someone (not specified as a friend) wanted to tell them what he or she believed about Christianity. The chances of finding a twenty- to twenty-nine-year-old not willing to listen is only one in ten, compared to one in four for those unchurched age thirty or better. However, it is still amazing that 75 percent of the older group would be willing to listen to someone tell them about Jesus! This represents an overwhelming majority and should thus be the focus of an intentional and relational strategy for outreach to these groups.

Willingness to study the Bible if a friend asked is only 42 percent among the older unchurched, compared to 61 percent for the younger group—a substantial difference. The Christian conversion of a friend would not be viewed positively among the thirty and older unchurched group. Nearly half of the younger unchurched agreed that if a friend expressed that he or she recently became a Christian, this would have a positive effect on their relationship.

The spiritual quest draws younger unchurched to learn more about Christianity, Jesus, and the Bible. They are no doubt open to non-Christian expressions of spirituality as well.

How Do Churches Connect with the Younger Unchurched?

If the younger unchurched are more open to spiritual things and more open to conversations about Christianity, they might also be more open to being influenced through outreach ministries. Comparing the two age groups makes a couple of things obvious: more study is needed on how to reach older unchurched adults, and the younger group is remarkably more receptive to the church.

Table 5: What Can Churches Do?	20–29	30+
If a church presented truth to me in an understandable way that relates to my life now, I would attend.	63%	47%
If people at church cared about me as a person, I would be more likely to attend.	58%	38%
I would be willing to join a small group of people to learn more about the Bible and Jesus.	46%	27%
If music at church sounded similar to my favorite type of music, I would be more likely to attend.	31%	26%

First, it should be noted that none of the four ideas for churches to reach out to the unchurched would impact a majority of the older unchurched. With all the talk of the loss of the younger generation, it seems to us that they are much more open than the older unchurched.

The younger unchurched need churches that present truth to them in a relevant way. They need churches that care about them as a person, and they need to be invited to join a small group to learn more about the Bible and Jesus. Just don't expect them to walk through the doors of church for 11:00 a.m. worship.

A Deeper Look at Spirituality

Earlier we established that the majority of the younger unchurched (72 percent) and the older cohort (67 percent) referred to themselves as spiritual. When asked their level of agreement with the statement, "I consider myself to be spiritual because I am interested in knowing more about God, or a higher supreme being," 73 percent of the unchurched in their twenties and 62 percent of those age thirty or older registered either strong or somewhat agreement.

Table 6: A Deeper Look at Spirituality	20–29	30+
I consider myself to be spiritual because I am interested in knowing more about God, or a higher supreme being.	73%	62%
Most of my friends are spiritual.	54%	61%
People who attend a Christian church are generally more spiritual than those who do not attend.	39%	27%

The most interesting comparison in Table 6 may be that the older group of unchurched agree more that most of their friends are spiritual. This older group pretty much discounts the notion that church attendance is an indicator of spirituality. In fact, this implies that their spiritual friends are not attending church either.

Heaven? and Hell?

The younger unchurched are substantially more aware of and concerned about eternity. Both surveys asked, "How often do you wonder, 'If I were to die today, would I go to heaven?'" The distribution of responses among the thirty and older group was 10 percent daily, 6 percent weekly, 12 percent monthly, 13 percent yearly, and 59 percent never or not sure.

These older folks may call themselves spiritual, but one thing is certain, they are not particularly worried about eternity. The continuation of a person's spirit in an afterlife is agreed to by 69 percent of the older unchurched compared to 82 percent of the younger.

Table 7: Heaven and Hell	20–29	30+
When a person dies, his or her spirit continues to exist in an afterlife.	82%	69%
There exists a place of reward in the afterlife, sometimes called heaven.	77%	58%
There exists a place of punishment in the afterlife, sometimes called hell.	60%	44%
My belief about the existence of an afterlife has an impact on the way I live.	63%	46%

The younger unchurched once again seem more ready to hear an evangelistic witness, since they are more likely than the older unchurched to believe in the existence of a place of reward and a place of punishment in the afterlife. Fewer than half of the older unchurched agreed that their belief about the afterlife has an impact on how they live.

Christianity

It seems that both age groups have similar views of the generic Christian religion. Both ages of unchurched respondents agree that Christianity is a relevant and viable religion. Yet, both were harsh in their judgment that Christianity is more about organized religion than loving God and people.

Table 8: Christianity	20–29	30+
The Christian religion is a relevant and viable religion for today.	74%	63%
I think Christianity today is more about organized religion than about loving God and loving people.	77%	83%

Searching for Guidance

A person seeking inspirational or spiritual guidance in today's culture has a plethora of choices. Survey participants were asked for one source they would consult: "Which of the following sources would you consult if you were seeking inspirational guidance?"

20 to 29	**30 and Over**	
• 41 percent	29 percent	would talk or listen to an inspirational person
• 22 percent	28 percent	would read an inspirational book
• 17 percent	17 percent	would go to church
• 8 percent	3 percent	would watch an inspirational movie
• 7 percent	3 percent	would search the Internet
• 5 percent	21 percent	were not sure what they would do

It is interesting to note that the younger unchurched would choose a more relational path (a person) with greater frequency, and the older would just as likely choose a book. The survey also asked specifically about television and the Internet as sources of spiritual guidance. Agreement levels with these two statements are given in Table 9.

Table 9: Spiritual Guidance	**20–29**	**30+**
I have searched for spiritual help online.	19%	9%
Sometimes I watch a Christian television program.	37%	40%

The older unchurched are less likely to turn to a person they think is inspirational. Also, more would prefer to read an inspirational book (maybe the Bible) rather than seek spiritual help from a church.

Remarkably and disturbingly, only one in six in either age group would go to church if seeking inspirational guidance. The church is simply not the first choice of the unchurched seeking inspirational guidance. However, one out of five older unchurched is not sure where she or he would turn in a time of crisis.

Christian television is watched sometimes by 40 percent of the older unchurched and a slightly lower amount among the younger unchurched. The younger are much more likely to search for spiritual help online. Only 9 percent of the older group has searched for spiritual help online.

Relating to Christians

Relationships with Christian friends and feelings toward Christians vary little by age group. In fact, older unchurched respondents were more likely to agree they had many Christian friends.

Table 10: Relationships with Christians	20–29	30+
I have at least one close friend who considers himself or herself a Christian.	91%	89%
I have many Christian friends.	69%	79%
Christians get on my nerves.	46%	44%

Nine out of ten unchurched American adults have at least one Christian among their close friends. This does not imply that the Christian friend is churched. Christians are equally irritating to both age groups, getting on the nerves of just under half of the unchurched.

Unlike the younger unchurched, having Christian friends does impact whether Christians get on the nerves of the older group. Having one close Christian friend *increases* agreement that Christians get on the older unchurched nerves (45 percent compared to 39 percent), but having many Christian acquaintances has the opposite effect. Forty-three percent of the older group with many Christian friends agreed that Christians get on their nerves, compared to 56 percent of those without multiple Christian friends.

Among the unchurched age thirty and older, groups with the most agreement that Christians irritate them include the college educated (51 percent), those currently in civil unions or domestic partnerships (74 percent), the thirty to fifty-four age subgroup (55 percent), and the atheist/humanist/realist subgroup (69 percent). Relatively few (16 percent) of African-Americans among this age group agree that Christians get on their nerves.

Conclusion

For both age groups, some significant concerns can be raised about basic beliefs. Neither group has a strong belief in the One, True, Living God of the Bible, nor a strong belief that He is unique compared to other gods. When reaching out to these age groups, this issue is something that needs to be taken into consideration. We live in a pluralistic society, and we need to expect that people, especially the younger generations, will have inclusive beliefs about who God is.

In addition, the younger and the older unchurched have a pretty low view of the church. In their view the church is too critical about lifestyle issues, full of hypocrites, and not necessary for spiritual development. However, both groups still believe that the church has a positive impact on society as a whole (almost 75 percent). That is something that churches can utilize to help build an effective strategy.

Here's the really good news! These groups clearly indicate they are willing to dialogue about Christianity and Jesus. We think it is fair to say that the younger unchurched (and the older unchurched to a slightly lesser degree) are more open to who God is and to hearing more about Him from Christians. This is an important finding in a time when Christians are unsure of how to relate to emerging generations.

— A LOST AND FOUND STORY CONTINUED —

Dean Carey stood at the sliding glass door leading out to the balcony of his fifth floor apartment and looked up the road in the direction from where Ally would be coming. He glanced at the Surround style clock resting on the glass end table nearby: 8:30. He would have been surprised if she'd made it by eight, but 30 minutes late was even a stretch for her. "Maybe she got hung up while dropping the Christmas gifts by the women's shelter," he thought.

About that time he felt the familiar buzz of his iPhone. He reached in his pocket and pulled it out to read a text message from Ally. "B thr n 10," it read.

"Ten minutes," he thought. "I've got just enough time for a small glass of wine. Glad I didn't go down and stand in the cold."

He finished his drink and took the elevator downstairs. He walked outside just as Ally whipped to the curb. He barely got the door open when he heard her.

"Don't say it, don't even start with me. I already know I'm going to hear it from Mitch first chance he gets. I'd bet money he'll even shoot a glance at his watch when he sees us walk in. He'll bring up every time transgression I've ever committed."

Dean knew for sure Mitch was going to bring it up. No way was he going to let a chance slide by to rib Ally for being late, especially this late. He also knew it would be good-natured. Some people might do that whole truth in jest thing and tease Ally for her tardiness, but really be annoyed by it. Dean never knew Mitch to be that way.

But that was the thing about Mitch. He just didn't seem to be arrogant toward anybody, which intrigued Dean. After all, nearly everybody he ever knew who went to church and claimed to be a Christian came off at least somewhat condescending, especially to a teenage boy who took more interest in clothing styles and the Thespian Club than in sports. Of course it's been years now since he'd been in church.

He was hardly paying attention to Ally prattle on as the memory of church put him mentally on the defensive. *It's not that I ever had a problem with God,* he thought. *In fact if anyone had ever taken the time to really talk to me, they'd have known that. It may have given me a chance to ask them why they think He's different from the gods of any other world religion.*

As Dean conversed in his head about church, he conceded that part of the reason he got defensive is how rejected he felt when some of the leaders found out he was a homosexual. Instead of experiencing the love that supposedly the Bible taught, all he got was a lecture on how his lifestyle was a sin and that he'd wind up in hell if he didn't repent and change. He still thinks about that but believes God is more gracious than hypocritical ministers.

Even today, at twenty-five, he sometimes struggles with his homosexuality. But he remembers being especially confused as a teenager. His father certainly wasn't going to talk to him about it. He never could do anything well enough to solicit an affirming comment from his father. His dad had been a real basketball jock and wanted his only son to be one too. It didn't turn out that way. Dean never gained an aptitude for basketball.

Dean became an overachiever, excelling in everything—except sports. Without that, he simply wasn't going to get validation from his father. Maybe that's why he cranks out 16-hour days at the marketing firm where he works. He's already been promoted twice, hopping peers who've been there at least four years longer than him. It's created jealousy and some backstabbing. But he doesn't care. Maybe it's not right, he often considers, but ultimately, the way he figures it the bosses are happy with his work, and he's happy with himself when they are happy with him.

He remembered the day two years ago when he first met Mitch. He'd swung by Starbucks to pick up Ally for dinner.

"Oh good, I'm glad you got here a little early," Ally had said. "You remember I told you about my friend Mitch. Well this is him. Mitch, this is my friend Dean I told you all about."

Dean tensed up at the memory and felt a flash of the panic he'd felt that day. Oh my God, what did she say about me? Did she tell him I'm gay? Is he going to unload on me like all the other Christians did back when I went to church?

He'd hoped his exterior demeanor belied the terror he felt inside, but in a split second he remembered being shocked, then relieved.

"Dean, it's good to finally meet you," Mitch said as he reached out his right hand and looked Dean square in the eyes. "Ally has told me so much about you." Mitch's genuineness pierced him to the soul.

Ally jerked the car into the Cozy Note's parking lot, and it jerked Dean back to the present. They bolted for the door, checked coats, and tried to look collected as they moved through the seated crowd toward the "friends table" in front of stage left. The thought of that first encounter was fresh on Dean's mind when he saw Mitch chuckle at their tardiness.

Just like Mitch to let it slide, thought Dean. It's hard to believe he's a Christian. He seems so real. I believe he does love me.

Dean glanced around, then down at his watch.

It's like us to be late, Dean thought, but it's not like Jacob. I wonder where he is.

Part 1 Wrap-Up

1. The four general types of younger unchurched we described are: *Always Unchurched, De-Churched, Friendly Unchurched,* and *Hostile Unchurched.*

2. Many younger unchurched value spiritual matters but say they are turned off by religion. When asked to describe their own personal religious or spiritual beliefs, 43 percent of the younger unchurched said they were spiritual but not religious. Another 31 percent claimed to be both spiritual and religious. Only 9 percent were religious but not spiritual, and 18 percent said they were neither spiritual nor religious. It is inaccurate to think that young adults do not consider themselves to be spiritual.

3. Forty percent of the young unchurched identify with a denomination or faith group.

4. More than 60 percent of the younger unchurched reported attending church weekly when they were growing up.

5. A majority (81 percent) of younger unchurched adults in America believe that God or a higher supreme being exists. But 58 percent believe the God of the Bible is no different from the gods or spiritual beings depicted by world religions such as Islam, Hinduism, or Buddhism.

6. More than 60 percent believe Jesus died and came back to life. The younger unchurched are open to the person of Jesus and are interested in Him.
7. Nearly three quarters expressed at least some level of agreement that the Christian church is generally helpful to society as a whole.
8. About nine out of ten younger unchurched believe they do not need the church in order to have a good relationship with God or to learn what it means to be a Christian.
9. Almost 90 percent of the unchurched twenty- to twenty-nine-year-olds said they would be willing to listen if someone wanted to tell them about Christianity.
10. Three out of five younger unchurched respondents agreed they would be willing to study the Bible if a friend asked them to do so.
11. More than 60 percent said they would attend a church if it presented truth in an understandable and relevant way.
12. Although the younger unchurched agree that Christianity is a relevant and viable religion, they also believe that Christianity is more about organized religion than loving God and people.
13. Only one in six would go to church if seeking inspirational guidance.

The Bad News: The younger unchurched believe the church is too critical about lifestyle issues, full of hypocrites, and not necessary for spiritual development.

The Good News: The younger unchurched clearly indicate they are willing to dialogue about Christianity and Jesus.

— PART 2 —

Listening

WE STARTED OUR EXPLORATION OF THE YOUNGER UNCHURCHED by evaluating some groundbreaking polling research. We asked the younger unchurched about their beliefs, ideas, and perceptions—and you have read the results of this research in Part 1.

We also wanted to understand the *values* of young adults. To achieve this goal, LifeWay undertook a study of young adults to learn more than just statistics. We used polling and one-on-one surveys to talk to more than five hundred (churched and unchurched combined, from interviews and polling data) young adults across the country in order to better understand their mind-sets and value systems.

The original research project lasted eight months and has been followed by additional research projects and new initiatives.

In the chapters that follow, we will share more of the discoveries we have made regarding young adults, their passions, and how to reach them; but we think it is essential that we know them before we seek to reach them.

Our research points to four markers of young adult ministry, based on their own responses.

Community is vital to the emerging generations. For them, life is meant to be experienced together, and they sense a need to be involved in genuine relationships with others. They are looking for friends they can call for help when their tire is flat and people who will call and celebrate when they get a promotion.

They want to walk through life with their friends. They have a need for people, and they show a deep desire for relational equity. In other words, they long to be deeply invested in others and have others deeply invest in them. They desire to be a major part of each other's lives—the day-to-day, big and small "stuff of life." They also think that others should be a part of the most important aspect of their lives—their spiritual journey.

Depth is important. Young adults want to be people of significance. Deep significance. They care about who they are and what they're becoming—"ankle deep" doesn't work for them. They told us that they'd rather be "in over their heads" in life as opposed to kicking around in the shallow end.

Young adults also have interest in addressing the hard-to-talk-about topics. They appreciate tough questions and despise pat answers. Their responses indicate they like wrestling with difficult things and chewing on challenging ideas. They express a high degree of interest in processing information, and they often find the questions more important than the answers.

Responsibility is strongly valued because young adults know their choices make a difference. Decisions are everywhere. Recycle. Buy or trade fair. Sponsor a child. Respect your elders. Tithe. Love your neighbors. Respond to the crisis in Darfur.

These are the type of opportunities that define this generation. They affirmed the importance of these issues, and they are committed to doing the "right" thing even as they grow in their understanding of what right means. They've concluded that all of these decisions matter, and what matters most is how they respond.

Connection is the fourth area of importance. This could be called mentoring or intergenerational ministry. They want to learn from those who have already experienced the things they are about to face.

They're looking for a connection with people who will walk alongside them and advise them. They want a connection that gives them the opportunity to have someone pour their lives into them and teach them along their journey. And interestingly enough, they're willing to do that for someone else too.

Let's now take a more in-depth look into what the younger unchurched believe about these four markers of community, depth, responsibility, and connection.

Marker #1:
Community

GOD EXISTS AS COMMUNITY. HE HAS IDENTIFIED HIMSELF FROM the outset as both a community and One who desires community. In the creation story we hear, "Let us make man in our image," signifying both His nature (He is community) and His intent (He created us for community).

The church has, for generations, spoken of community. However, most of us would agree that community has been more of an aspiration than a reality. We have "aspired" to build community, but it has scarcely been realized. And that has not gone unnoticed by young adults, both inside and outside the church.

My youngest daughter learns in kindergarten, "They will know we are Christians by our love." My fourth grader reminds me, "By this men will all know that you are my disciples, if you love one another." Yet, these verses that call for community are not often lived out in our lives. But community is a central value for young adults, whether secular or sacred. Churched and unchurched alike are desperate for it.

Research—What Did We Learn?

As we interviewed individuals across the country, we were committed to capturing everything that was discussed. We didn't want to miss anything. We recorded every conversation and took extensive notes. After each interview the recorded conversation was transcribed into manuscript form. From that point each manuscript was evaluated and reviewed in depth to discover the major themes and points of significance. As we lifted the content from the transcripts, each major statement was placed on a Post-it note. Before we knew it, hundreds upon hundreds of Post-it notes had appeared—a common approach when doing qualitative research.

Next, we started to group the notes into large, general categories. As frequencies appeared and increased and similar responses surfaced, we identified new groupings. Finally, after concluding this process, we went back through our notes and identified the one note that most accurately identified the sentiments of the larger group. The statements on those notes were termed "key images." You will see those key images below to help you visualize what this phase of the process looked like. They all speak of community.

Key Images

Key Image: There's No Place Like Home

- *"Being in a home is a different atmosphere—we're all just sitting around the table eating dinner and catching up."*
- *"I want a place I can call my own and be a part of. I want to be heard and nurtured in an environment where you know someone enough that you're not ashamed to ask for something."*
- *"Worship draws us together and small groups keep us together."*

— WHAT STANDS OUT —

- An interest in casual, authentic encounters
- A desire for relational equity through both presence and programs
- An obvious desire to both listen to and process content
- A desire for relationships that go beyond "hello" and "hi"

Key Image: We're Family

- *"I'm hungry to be known intimately and to be challenged."*
- *"I'll say liturgy all day if someone will understand my pain."*
- *"The greeter said, 'I don't know you' and gave her a hug. She just cried as she took her seat. It was the first hug she'd had in a year."*

— WHAT STANDS OUT —

- An interest in both equity and accountability in relationships
- A greater interest in relationship than church programs
- A general longing for companionship and/or friendships
- A desire to process hurts or frustrations with others

Key Image: I'm All Alone in the Crowd

- *"We all have crazy schedules. When we do get together, it's a miracle."*
- *"Young adults are searching with an unsettled feeling, almost like a nomad."*
- *"Who am I going to call whenever I have an immediate need or who am I going to call whenever I want to go to Starbucks?"*

— WHAT STANDS OUT —

- An apparent schedule challenge that combats community
- A stage of exploration and discovering new things
- A desire for relationships that are available despite the circumstances

Key Image: Show Me the Real Thing

- *"I walked into church with baggage—church burnout, tired of games, pointing out hypocrites, overly programmed."*
- *"It was boring—dead. I just wanted to say, 'You're up there singing about the joy of the Lord and you look like you are at a funeral.'"*

— WHAT STANDS OUT —

- A possible poor experience with the church in the past
- A dislike of both programming and some people within the church
- A desire for a connection to personal conviction and authenticity

Key Image: You Don't Fit, So We Don't Care

- *"Young adults are in the middle—not old enough, not in high school—you are at this 'ugh' stage."*
- *"After graduation they give you a pat on the back and say, 'When you start a family we'll be here for you.'"*

— WHAT STANDS OUT —

- A transitional season of life that may seem awkward for some
- An apparent desire by some churches to only connect with one group of young adults

Key Image: You're Struggling. I'm Struggling. No Games.

- *"We can't have any kind of good Bible study if people aren't being real."*
- *"What draws people is a climate of honesty. We don't come to hide from each other and put on masks and give all trick answers and Sunday school answers."*
- *"That's the first time I had ever seen what doing life with Jesus day to day looked like. I saw people with their knees in the dirt—they didn't have it all together. They had their problems too."*

— WHAT STANDS OUT —

- A belief that quality is greatly contingent upon transparency
- Honesty and vulnerability may help in both reaching and keeping young adults
- An interest in seeing a relationship with Jesus lived out in everyday life
- A desire to address and be open about the struggles of life

Together Is Better

Key Image: There's No Place Like Home

Key Image: We're Family

Key Image: I'm All Alone in the Crowd

Key Image: Show Me the Real Thing

Key Image: You Don't Fit, So We Don't Care

**Key Image: You're Struggling.
I'm Struggling. No Games.**

Statistics

After the face-to-face interviews and online polling, we found that the quantitative research seemed to effectively capture the ideas expressed in the qualitative research. Clearly this was encouraging. This not only validated the research, but it also led us to believe that we were getting real answers to some of our questions. Maybe, just maybe, we were on to something. Here's what stood out related to the topic of community:

- Among unchurched adults, 58 percent of younger adults (ages eighteen to twenty-nine) are more likely to attend church if people at church cared for them as compared to 38 percent of older adults (thirty years and older).[1]
- Seventy-three percent of church members and 47 percent of nonaffiliated young adults indicated that community with other young adults is extremely important in their lives.
- Forty-six percent of unchurched young adults indicate that exploring religious environments without pressure is important or very important.

These statistics continue to show the desire of young adults, both churched and unchurched, to find community with other people. Through a detailed analysis of the findings above, and with numerous other statistics we have gleaned from the data, we have drawn some rather significant conclusions:

- Young adults, both churched and unchurched, indicated that having the opportunity to interact with members of a group multiple times per week was very important.
- Young adults, both churched and unchurched, desire to participate in a maximum number of small group activities that promote relationship/belonging.
- Unchurched young adults desire to explore the church environment with a minimum amount of pressure for commitment.

Analysis (What Does It Mean?)

Together Is Better

Young adults clearly express a sincere longing to be part of deep, authentic community. Quite simply, they were saying that *together is better.*

Unfortunately dysfunctional communities are the ones that have gained the most notoriety in our culture. As a result, for many, our ideas of "normal" community are distorted. Mental images (or first-hand memories) arise of peace, love, and LSD when we think about community. David Koresh or Warren Jeffs and their religious sects may come to mind, and our first reaction toward the word *community* might be to recoil.

To clarify the imagery and meaning, the most common use of the word *community* indicates a sizeable group of people living in close proximity, a geographic community. In other instances, "community" might indicate a group of people with a common identity other than location. Members interact regularly around a common belief, practice, or affinity. A good example is a professional community or even a virtual community. In other instances, overlap occurs when members choose to live near each other because of one or more of their common interests. This is seen in an Amish community or an ecovillage.[2]

This "living near" can be a close physical proximity to one another, or it may be a relational closeness. In most cases, it means both.

Emerging generations are searching for the security provided by relationships with like-minded people, forming a family bond by friendship rather than kinship. You might find a group of young adults living life together, closer than a family. Emerging generations "long to belong" and are hungry for a *we*-centered approach to growing spiritually, rather than a *me*-centered approach.

Implications (What Should We Do?)

The Early and Late Church

The desire for community is good news for the church because community is central to its mission. So, it is fair to say, especially in today's context, that spiritual growth doesn't take place outside of community. In Scripture we see something similar expressed:

> They devoted themselves to the apostles' teaching and to the fellowship, to the breaking of bread and to prayer. Everyone was filled with awe, and many wonders and miraculous signs were done by the apostles. All the believers were together and had everything in common. Selling their possessions and goods, they gave to anyone as he had need. Every day they continued to meet together in the temple courts. They broke bread in their homes and ate together with glad and sincere hearts, praising God and enjoying the favor of all the people. (Acts 2:42–47)

But what does that look like today?

The foundational premise of community is that life is meant to be experienced together. Community is about intimately journeying through life with those who surround you. That may be found, to some degree, with those that live across the globe but will more likely be found among those you personally interact with on a regular basis. Truth be told—we need one another.

Again, this is good news for Christianity, a religion built on relationships with God and others. You can't buy community, program community, or fake community. *It's the reality of the relationships that makes Christ believable to an unbelieving society. The person far from God will not come to Christ until the love of Christ annihilates the opposing worldview upon which they depend.* Community is the love of God manifesting itself in and through the people of God.

More Than Coffee

Maybe the only thing that young adults desire as much as community is coffee. They are the men and women who not only like coffee, but they know everything about it. They have definite preferences in their coffee brand, and they are quite comfortable throwing around terms like "Venti Mocha" and "Iced Americano."

Perhaps that's why Starbucks has the appeal it does. Most young adults have Starbucks as part of their experience—many of them even work there from time to time. But interestingly enough, many young adults will say that Starbucks isn't the best coffee they've ever had.

But, obviously, Starbucks is doing pretty well. Granted their stock values have fluctuated, but there still seems to be one on just about every corner. In addition, their products are sold in grocery stores all across the Unites States and Canada. So, how can this be? Starbucks is highly successful, yet they don't necessarily sell the best coffee on the market.

Starbucks is successful because it sells more than coffee. It sells community. In their stores they intentionally create environments by design and acoustics that encourage conversations, comfort, and accessibility. Beyond their stores, they are selling products that are ideal to be used in community-friendly settings. This is not by accident. Starbucks spends millions of dollars each year executing their *third place* strategy.

Starbucks CEO Howard Schultz has said, "We're in the business of human connection and humanity, creating communities in a third place between home and work." In his influential book *The Great, Good Place*, Ray Oldenburg argues that third places are important for civil society, democracy, civic engagement, and establishing feelings of a sense of place. Oldenburg calls one's "first place" the home and those with whom one lives. The "second place" is the workplace—where people may actually spend most of their time. "Third places," then, are "anchors" of community life and facilitate and foster broader, more creative interaction.[3]

Starbucks is selling something that has more appeal and demand than any product they could ever place on their menu. Most coffee drinkers love their favorite beverage, but Starbucks is aware that those very same people may possibly be craving something else as well. And may I be the first (or 50 millionth) person to say this, but their strategy is genius. I don't even drink coffee, yet I catch myself attending meeting after meeting at various Starbucks around the country. I also spend countless hours writing or working in various Starbucks's locations just because I feel the need to be in an authentic, creative, and thought-provoking environment.

This type of strategy capitalizes on a fundamental need that exists within our society, especially for younger adults. They want to do life together. They want to go beyond the causal "hellos" of life and go deeper in their relationships with one another. They are looking for intimate, personal relationships.

As mentioned previously, this interest in community applies to both Christians and those who don't claim to have a relationship with Jesus. The younger unchurched, specifically, identified this as a major factor in their interest toward church and what they might find appealing in their search for one. They were looking to live life alongside each other, far beyond the parameters of any church building. We have an amazing opportunity to meet that need as we align our churches with what we are already called to be—a hub for authentic, deep community.

Some Reminders and a Must

The community young adults are looking for is similar to what has been described. Here's a list of desired characteristics:

- Community should encourage honesty, authenticity, and freedom to ask questions.
- Community should endorse a connection between one's actions and their personal convictions.
- Community should minimize church jargon.
- Community should provide an atmosphere where it's OK to not know all the answers.
- Community should be full of personal illustrations and life applications.[4]

It's also important to differentiate between our need to provide a God-honoring community and what the secular world might be seeking. At the end of the day, we're not just looking to grow people closer to one another for the sake of communal improvement and general happiness. The bottom line "must" of community, as we're describing in this chapter, has the foundational purpose of developing people into growing followers of Jesus. Why? Because we are "in Christ" and our lives are "hidden in Him," as such, being in community with us introduces them to community with God through Jesus.

A healthy relationship with God doesn't disqualify you from a healthy relationship with others, nor do healthy relationships with others disqualify you from a healthy relationship with God. The two should coexist in your life. According to Scripture, it is wrong for them to be mutually exclusive from each other. In 1 John 4:11–12, the writer declares, "Dear friends, since God so loved us, we also ought to love one another. No one has ever seen God; but if we love one another, God lives in us and his love is made complete in us." Thus, as individuals grow closer to one another in healthy, biblical community, they are also growing closer to the Father. This is the biblical model.

Our friends at McLean Bible Church in the Washington, D.C., area describe community appropriately:

> True biblical community is more than just having Christian
> friends. It is a spiritual discipline focused on helping
> one another become fully devoted followers of Christ. It
> involves relational intimacy, transparency, vulnerability
> and accountability. Romans 12:5 tells us, "so in Christ, we
> (believers) who are many form one body, and each member
> belongs to all the others." As with our physical body, so it
> is with the body of Christ—when one part suffers, all suffer.
> God has designed and gifted our fellow believers in Jesus
> Christ to perform unique and vital services to help you. Some
> of these services include being devoted to one another, serving
> one another, accepting one another, instructing one another,
> bearing one another's burdens, forgiving one another,
> comforting one another, encouraging one another, and
> looking out for the interests of others, just to name a few![5]

The Challenges of Community

So younger adults are looking for community. But simply having that desire doesn't make it easy to establish, does it? Creating an environment that is conducive to the development of community is difficult. To do that, a church must walk the fine line between being programmatic and organic, between being institutional and relational, and between being rigid and flexible. A number of challenges make it difficult to foster biblical, God-honoring community.

CHALLENGE #1: TECHNOLOGY

It may be strange to talk technology while talking about community, but technology has become a leading tool for community.

Let's face it, most young adults carry enough electronic devices with them to power a microwave.

Technology was intended to make our world more convenient and allow us to communicate more easily. Without a doubt, we are more accessible and more connected over greater distances than ever before.

The primary challenge associated with technology is that all too often we replace authentic conversation and much needed face-to-face interaction with iChats and instant messaging sessions. We choose convenience over intimacy, and technology is the avenue that allows it to happen. *Churches must find the balance that allows them to use technology for the development of community while not allowing it to replace community.*

CHALLENGE #2: VELOCITY

It doesn't matter if you live in a downtown metropolis or in rural America; it's probably safe to say that you have your share of instances when you feel like you can't keep up with the rapid pace of things. We're doing everything possible to keep up with the pace—whether it's getting to our next meeting, knocking out that assignment, picking up the kids, etc. It's amazing how many things compete for time and attention. Interwoven in this challenge are the notions of convenience and instant gratification. The idea of waiting is foreign to most of you. You can get your #4 combo at McDonald's in two minutes—any longer is unacceptable. You can drop off your dry cleaning in the morning and have it back that afternoon. We have the ability to access an unending stream of data and information through the Internet at an amazing pace. Unfortunately community doesn't work this way. It takes time and commitment. You don't establish that level of connectivity overnight.

Groups seeking to build relationships among young adults will not be short-term study groups but rather longer term commitments before becoming true communities with trust and intimacy. A key to evangelizing emerging generations is the presence of Christian community. But that sense must be cultivated in a lengthy, often messy process of transparency and vulnerability.

CHALLENGE #3: SECURITY

Another major challenge to building community is security. We live in a world where we are bombarded by headlines of terrorism, fraud, murder, lawsuits, and lies. We have become cautious and cynical when meeting strangers and have learned to keep our distance from those we meet. In a time of serial rapists, sexual predators, school shootings, and Amber alerts, this is understandable, but it's a barrier to building community.

So it's simply not enough to start a Bible study and extend an invitation. Jesus used a "come and see" strategy. Churches reaching young adults are inviting people to experience life together (it's *better* that way), not to a program. They're allowing the spiritual journey to begin before conversion. Spiritual seekers are invited to participate in the faith community before they share the faith. Allowing someone to belong doesn't mean that he or she is incorporated into the body of Christ. It means they're seeking a safe place to be.

But safety can only be achieved through intimacy. And the uncomfortable reality is that intimacy is give and take. Security is created only when people inside a community are willing to disclose the hidden parts of who they are. Ironically, to create security, we must first be willing to step into a great deal of insecurity.

CHALLENGE #4: FAMILY AND RELATIONAL DYSFUNCTION

One final challenge worth noting is the prevalence of family dysfunction. Divorce rates are high and single-parent homes are becoming more the norm. Parental presence has been absent in many young people's lives. This is not always a result of marital strife or even death within a family unit. In many cases young adults were simply ignored or mistreated by their parents. These circumstances do impact the context in which individuals approach community. Quite simply, if a young adult never saw community modeled in his or her own home as a child, that has a huge impact on their efforts to gain community as an adult.

Where Challenge Meets Opportunity

Within these challenges to community, incredible opportunity resides as well. By engaging these challenges, we can actually turn them on their heads as a means of creating community rather than hindering it.

TECHNOLOGY

Technology is here to stay. If that's the case, we must learn to use it to our advantage in order to better engage today's generations. Recognizing that young adults are somewhat nomadic and extraordinarily busy, our ability to communicate with one another must not rest exclusively on the shoulders of face-to-face interaction. Does this contradict what has previously been said? No, it doesn't.

A big difference exists between using a tool like technology to strengthen communication, as opposed to allowing it to become the sole vehicle that sustains it. We highly recommend utilizing tools like Facebook, blogs, Twitter, and instant messaging to stay in touch. This doesn't apply only to social networking or catching up, either. Utilize technology to encourage spiritual growth also.

A few ways to consider using technology to create opportunities:

- Start a blog
- Have a private community for the church family
- Text prayer requests
- Be on Facebook and MySpace
- Podcast your messages
- Put text message moments in your sermons
- Have people instant-message questions for discussion during the service

There are countless other opportunities. But be sure of this, technology will continue to play a huge role in the life of young adults. Don't be shy about finding ways to use it.

Velocity

Although it is increasingly difficult to slow down and move beyond surface conversations with other people, young adults are looking for opportunities to do just that. As previously mentioned, instant access and immediate gratification abound. But our lives don't always work that way, do they? We have major events taking place in our lives that demand time, emotional energy, and heavy analysis. And this is often experienced within the comforts of relational community. It is found in times of discussion, interaction, and possibly even prayer.

A huge opportunity exists here. Better yet, this is not something that today's church thought up on its own. This is a biblical mandate. If the church can nurture community in a way that allows this type of exploration, it will find itself providing one of the very things that younger adults are looking for the most. So we have a biblical mandate that coincides with a cultural need—an opportunity for God to work in powerful ways.

In the end, people have time to do what they desire to do. The great difficulty is developing a sense of community that is so appealing that people will make time to be a part of it. Right now few will choose a small group meeting over coffee at Starbucks or their child's Little League ball game. We must seek ways to develop an expression of community that is so powerful that people would rather be there than anywhere else.

SECURITY

Safety and security will be forefront issues for the rest of our lives. Therefore, if we seek to provide environments that are both physically and emotionally safe for individuals, then we will increase the chances that the younger unchurched will be drawn to us, our ministries, and possibly our churches.

Central characteristics of being a Christ follower, such as honesty, integrity, and selflessness, will become increasingly attractive in a world that is guarded, skeptical, and jaded. In addition, each church's ability to create this type of environment rests heavily upon the shoulders of its leadership. If you never offer vulnerability or availability to people, they will likely remain disengaged as well.

If we can develop relationships that withstand personality flaws and allow people to drop their guard and become honest, then we can make some progress. But will this generation be tempted to move on once they are challenged to address their flaws? On the other hand, older generations often suffer from serial relationships that are shallow—saying they want relationship but not sure how to do it. So, will the older generations embrace true community or run when things start getting transparent?

FAMILY AND RELATIONAL DYSFUNCTION

Young adults are looking for deep, family-like relationships. For some, this is something they have never had in the past. For others, they just long for more significant, healthy relationships. If the body of Christ will provide opportunities for these types of relationships to develop with this generation, the doors of evangelism and life-changing ministry could be flung wide open.

A Paradigm Shift

For years too many churches, intentionally or unintentionally, have functioned with a behave/believe/belong ministry model. This approach toward the unchurched has been one that began by connecting with those that behaved in a certain way. Sadly our openness to the unchurched is often based more on the outward "acceptable" behaviors rather than our call to reach them. We too often focus on moralizing the unconverted rather than reaching those who need Christ. This doesn't necessarily mean the individual's behavior was pleasant or edifying, but it was somehow deemed as acceptable by man.

After discovering a person's behavior, the church then explored the individual's beliefs. Only after a person's behaviors and beliefs were accepted was the door to belonging finally opened. Sadly, until that point, community was not made available. We must change this model. It is becoming increasingly less effective.

Rather than behave/believe/belong ministry, we must move toward a belong/believe/become model. What this means is that an unchurched individual is immediately welcomed into the community with other Christians. As previously stated, this doesn't mean incorporating someone as a new member of your church. Rather, it means creating an environment of acceptance for the unchurched despite their flaws and their unfamiliarity with the things of God and His church.

As we establish loving relationships and gain relational equity with the unchurched, then we are afforded the opportunity to teach them God's Word and to allow it to infiltrate what they believe. As this occurs, they will relationally and gradually become who God desires them to be.

— A LOST AND FOUND STORY CONTINUED —

Jacob Runion was a hard driver, type A all the way. Some might call him a "seek and destroy" kind of guy. He liked power of all kinds and at the moment was powering his way through city streets in his 2007 Grabber Orange Mustang GT. He pulled an all-nighter and lay down after dropping the final paper for his international relations class by his professor's office earlier in the afternoon. A 15-minute "power nap" turned into a six-hour nap, and now he was late.

What made him most angry wasn't that he was late—although he was pretty chapped by that—it was that he was sure he was going to be later than Ally, and the last thing he wanted to do was listen to her go on about "Mr. Always On Time" not being on time. The thought of it transferred from mind to accelerator. The verbal sparing with Ally was both enjoyable and frustrating—sometimes both at the same time. He liked Ally. They dated for nearly two years near the end of college, but they simply couldn't continue in a dating relationship the way they went at it. Besides, she went off to Africa with the Peace Corps, and he went to Washington, D.C. He shook his head. These were two opposites that didn't attract.

He'd often called Ally a "liberal, tree-hugging socialist," and she called him a "warmonger." He actually kind of liked the moniker because he played to it to aggravate her. He did believe a strong U.S. military presence was needed globally to enhance America's diplomatic positions. His views were shaped growing up overseas, the son of a foreign diplomat. He often heard his father crack after hanging up the phone with a country's representative that had said, "You'll either do it the easy way or the hard way. The easy way is to give us what we want."

Jacob liked living the life of a diplomat. It was a good life, a cushy life. But perks aside, he truly did have an interest in politics and government, which is why he majored in political science and was now close to finishing his master's in international relations. The two graduations were separated by a two-year internship with the State Department in Washington, D.C. It certainly helped having a father with some connections there. He also had his dad to thank for his current mode of transportation.

As he careened through the city streets toward the Cozy Note, Jacob thought about the irony. He was going to meet a girl he no longer dated, to listen to a band fronted by a guy he thought was a loafer, and looked forward to seeing a guy he thought was a religious fanatic. He laughed at the image.

"I gotta get out and meet some new people," he said out loud.

In fairness, he no longer thought of Mitch as a religious fanatic, although he still thought Mitch was somewhat extreme in his views. Over the past four years he'd slowly grown to respect Mitch. Whereas he could set Ally off with a comment or two, it was much harder to provoke Mitch, and he really wanted to, but Mitch rarely took the bait. He'd tried the first time they'd met. Mitch had been Ally's statistics tutor the year before but still came by Starbucks where Ally worked to hang out and talk after she got off work. Jacob and Ally had started dating that fall semester, and he walked in while they were talking about social work and the role churches play—or should play—in alleviating suffering around the world. Forty-five seconds after being introduced, Jacob went for the jugular.

"Alleviate suffering?" Jacob asked with a sarcastic tone. "How 'bout causes suffering. There has been more suffering caused around the world in the name of religion than anything else. From what I've seen growing up overseas, religion benefits a few of the biggies financially and the rest blindly follow being fed lines about how this god or that god will bestow

favor in exchange for devotion. Go to this country, it's Buddha. Go to that one, it's Allah. Come here, it's Jesus. You can't tell the gods apart without a scorecard. Everybody is claiming theirs is the real deal and that he is a god of peace. The only problem is they'll kill you to get you to believe it."

"Wow, you've got a lot going on there," Mitch said calmly. "I would disagree with much of what you said, but in many ways you are fundamentally right. The church historically has been the cause of much suffering."

Silence.

Jacob didn't know what to say. He saw Ally out of the corner of his eye lean back in her chair and cross her arms. A look of surprised satisfaction came across her face. Jacob had a quick mind, deep opinions, and liked to intellectually bury people, but he had no idea how to respond to Mitch. A couple seconds of silence passed, but it seemed like a week. He opened his mouth to mount a counter offensive.

"What?"

It was all he could muster.

"I believe you are combining two issues in your statement," Mitch replied. "The first is basically all gods are the same. I believe you're wrong on that one, and I'd love to discuss that with you sometime. But the second issue is the more prominent issue in your statement and that is that there has been much suffering done to humanity in the name of religion, and I'd specifically state in the name of Christianity. To that part of your statement I'd totally agree. And to that all I can say is I'm sorry. That part of Christian history is an embarrassment to the Christian faith and I believe totally out of step with what Jesus expects of His followers."

Even now, several years later, remembering that encounter with Mitch still left Jacob dumbfounded. He could guarantee that if Mitch had responded like every other Christian he'd intellectually dismantled, he wouldn't be pulling up to the valet stand tonight at the Cozy Note.

He hurried in, checked his black wool overcoat, grabbed a beer at the bar, and slipped through the crowd on his way to the table. He looked up at Mitch, mouthed, "Sorry." Mitch smiled, then twitched his head sideways as if to point in Ally's direction. Yeah, Jacob knew he was about to hear it, and he knew Mitch would probably take satisfaction in it.

The sight of Jacob gave Mitch a burst of enthusiasm as he popped his bass strings a little harder. He knew Ally and Dean would come, but wasn't so sure about Jacob. He was sometimes a hard read, but seeing him made the challenge of the past four years worth the effort.

And it had been quite a challenge. Still was.

5

Marker #2:
Depth (and Content)

IN 2005 I WAS A CONSULTANT FOR, AND A PARTICIPANT IN, A one-hour documentary on the church in emerging generations. The video (available now at amazon.com) was entitled, "The Changing Face of Worship." It aired on every ABC station in the country as their Christian season documentary on faith issues for that year.

The narrator, Rebecca Saint James, told the story of churches engaging people in emerging culture, with examples from each of the churches and their pastors. Darrell Guder (Princeton), Ryan Bolger (Fuller Seminary), Len Sweet (Drew University), and I (along with others) provided commentary through interviews.

Most churches were chosen based on research I had done a couple of years earlier. They represented different denominations and some different theological systems. However, one trait was consistent among all of these churches. They were spending more time and going deeper into the content of Scripture and theology than was common in more established churches. Content and depth were a passion.

Think for a moment about the childhood activity of dodgeball. Nothing screams fun and character building like blasting one another with oversized balls while everyone else points and laughs. If you played as a kid, you'll remember the experience well—the intentional swerving, the impulsive ducking, and the constant side-stepping. It was fun. Sadly these motions also seem to describe many of our churches today as they interact with truth and this generation. And young adults, churched and unchurched, have been taking notice. Those churched young adults, who are willing to stand for truth in today's culture, desire to be equipped. On the other hand, unchurched young adults also established that if they were ever to make a decision for Christ, then it would be an informed, educated one. Quite simply, they are proving the importance of depth and content by avoiding the churches that lack it.

Research (What Did We Learn?)

The findings related to this chapter's topic were derived by following the same research process discussed in previous chapters. It is also worth noting that the twenty-two attributes, described in the Attribute Importance section of our survey, came in large part from statements that we had heard in the face-to-face interview section of our research. By incorporating this information into our ongoing research, we had a greater opportunity to hear and learn more about specific issues that were being revealed as significant.

However, it is also worth noting that we did not eliminate the opportunity for new trends to surface in the ongoing collection of data. In both the polling and interviews, we provided an opportunity for respondents and interviewees to share other thoughts about matters of importance. Although not every person chose to provide this type of additional information, many did so, and their responses have played an important role in helping us arrive at the conclusions we are presenting in this part of the book.

Key Images

The intent of the "key images" section is to help you grasp a more accurate understanding of the qualitative aspect of our research. But, more importantly, it is here to reconnect you to the idea that all of this is about people—young adult people. We don't start research projects just for kicks. This is hard work and requires significant amounts of time, personnel, and money. Besides the actual acquisition of data, the process of interpreting it is extraordinarily complicated. But here's the bottom line—it's worth it. Research provides data, and data tells us about the very people we are seeking to reach. It helps us understand their opinions, needs, and so much more. Take a minute to hear "the voice of the people" as it's expressed in print through the following key images.

Key Image: Let Me Safely Join the Conversation

- *"It's not one person with all the answers. Rather, it's about all the people with their combined knowledge and experience."*
- *"I was afraid they'd be over my head because I felt uneducated about the Bible and religious things."*

— WHAT STANDS OUT —

- A desire to process and personalize content
- A recognition that everyone has something to contribute
- An interest in learning that provides entry points for people at all levels of spiritual maturity
- A genuine interest in God and the Bible
- An affinity toward discussion, struggle, and story

Key Image: Help Me Find My Way

- *"There is a lot of pressure from our society about making money, providing for your family, and being able to afford a home and a certain lifestyle. I think all those internal pressures started to collide with me, and they also collided with my faith."*
- *"Young adults are searching for truth that helps them live well on a daily basis."*
- *"I want to know who I am, but I'm not sure."*

— WHAT STANDS OUT —

- A strong desire to connect Scripture, faith, and real world issues
- An ongoing evaluation of one's personal beliefs, values, and lifestyle
- A strong desire for stability in a world that seems to be counteracting it
- A search for truth that impacts everyday living

Key Image: Young Adults Want the Real Truth

- *"I want a Bible study that actually teaches me the Bible."*
- *"Hands-on learning is always better for me."*
- *"There is so much use of church jargon. What is all that?"*
- *"Let's deal with the tough questions, and pat answers won't work."*

— WHAT STANDS OUT —

- A desire to address controversial topics in community
- A need to focus on truth and not what has been added to it
- An interest in exploring the Bible, including the challenging parts
- An examination of worldview and other forms of truth

Let's Go Deeper

Key Image: Let Me Safely Join the Conversation

Key Image: Help Me Find My Way

Key Image: Young Adults Want the Real Truth

Statistics

As previously mentioned, our survey contained three major sections. Although we gleaned the large majority of our data from those three sections, it's also important to remember that we surveyed one other section—the participant's background. At first glance this may seem insignificant, but it actually provided some important affirmation regarding the needs of this generation.

In short, we asked about people's sex, if they were married, if they had kids, if they were a full-time student, about their church involvement (or lack of), and several other basic questions. Our goal in seeking this information was primarily to be sure that we were gaining a complete and accurate understanding of young adults as a whole. And though some obvious social differences exist between the many different people in the eighteen- to thirty-four-year-old demographic, it was interesting to see that their overall thoughts about God and the church were similar. Here are some of their thoughts about content and depth:

- Following community, the second most important desire among young adult churchgoers is participation in small-group meetings to discuss life application of Scripture (71 percent).
- Forty-six percent of the non-regular church attendees desired to explore a religious environment without pressure. (This was the number one requirement of the unchurched.)
- Sixty-seven percent of churched young adults identified Bible studies about foundational Christian truths to be either important or very important.
- The unchurched indicated that only 14 percent of a possible study time should be dedicated to teacher explanation or lecture as opposed to 40 percent for discussion and hands-on learning.

As you can see, the statistical data we received through polling confirmed what we had heard in our conversations with young adults across the country. By combining this polling data and those interviews, we arrived at the following conclusions:

- Both churchgoers and the unchurched say that they desire to participate in Bible study that minimizes offering pat answers in the exploration of Scripture.

- Young adults desire to determine their own beliefs through a maximum of hands-on, practical learning experiences.
- Young adults desire to participate in small group meetings to discuss life application of Scripture with a maximum frequency.
- Young adults desire to have opportunities to participate in Bible study regarding a maximum number of foundational Christian truths.

Analysis (What Does It Mean?)

The Nonmodern Content

Content is an ambiguous term that is difficult to define and pin down, especially when referring to emerging generations. In one sense, everything has content, but the sort of content young adults seek is vastly different in its quality compared to what has been effective for previous generations.

Some of that difference can be explained in the divergence between the terms *modern* and *postmodern*. By its very definition, the era that has become known as *postmodernism* is against or after modernism. To fully grasp postmodernism and define the kind of content we are talking about in this chapter, we have to first examine what it is not.

Maybe the most definitive characteristic of the modern era has been logic. This was the era spawned by the Enlightenment and the Industrial Revolution. As humanity began to apply increased measures of reason and logic to its daily problems, we began to move toward regarding reason and logic with more and more respect. It became true in terms of science, but it also became true in spirituality.

Modernism was an era when books like *Evidence That Demands a Verdict* and *More Than a Carpenter* flourished because if you could *prove* that Christianity was true logically, then a person would have no choice but to accept. Evidentiary apologetics was the order of the day. But we are now in a day that is "postmodern," a day when people are tired of the modern belief that everything can be answered by science and reason. Consequently, especially in terms of content and depth, emerging generations often learn differently. They have a different epistemology—a different way to gain and measure knowledge.

Others have already noted that emerging generations are increasingly interested in a faith that embraces the mystical and spiritual. They are hungry for the unanswerable and want to connect with something that they cannot explain. I believe that this partially explains the impulse where many want to know *more* but are not seeking to know *fully*.

Maybe that became part of the problem with the church in the last couple of centuries. We forgot that it's not always about having a neat, pat answer. God gave us Jesus, and He gave us His Word. However, He did not give us all of the answers. And many sermons over the last few decades seemed to show that God and His plan could be wrapped up in thirty minutes just like a modern sitcom.

In many ways this is what Christianity has always been about. Faith by its very nature is illogical—it is the belief in the hilariously impossible. You might even go so far as to say that to reduce faith to a strictly empirical, formulaic system is to remove the trust element from it. Young adults seek depth, not pat answers.

Thus, trying to develop a neat and tidy systematic theology from a book that is a collection of God-inspired stories and letters can be counterintuitive to the spirit of the Bible. The challenge of Scripture is that it is often not systematic or logical. It is faith-oriented and obedience-based. In our thirst for knowledge presented in a systematic way, we have at times lost the miraculous and the demand for obedience. We have focused so intently on acquiring knowledge that we have sometimes misplaced the mystery of faith and the radical obedience required of Christ followers.

Good and Bad

Unfortunately this desire to connect with the spiritual and mystical have also led to the exploration and embracing of everything from astrology, New Age, tarot cards, psychics, ESP, channeling spirits, reincarnation, witchcraft, palm reading, UFOs and aliens, mother earth, crystal power, and Eastern or African spirituality. But the unifying characteristic in all of these expressions of spirituality is the desire to connect with something bigger than you are—something you believe yet cannot fully understand.

Young adults are looking for something more realistic—something that allows real challenges, real struggle, and real examination. An undeniable trend that showed up in our research is this desire and need for depth. This is revealed in both our research of younger adults and also in our study of ministries effectively reaching them. This level of depth, as described by younger adults, is characterized by a continual pursuit of knowledge, experience, wisdom, intellect, understanding, and exploratory learning. This type of discovery is thrusting individuals into the realms of academia, culture, and even spirituality. Both churched and unchurched younger adults identify faith matters and spirituality as matters of significant interest.

As we heard in our interviews, the spiritual interest that young adults expressed is not limited to things of Christianity. In fact, spirituality ranged from being something very abstract for some to something very specific for others. It was personal for some and yet, not at all for others. Also, spirituality was associated with a certain religion for some, and again, for others it was not. And finally, spirituality had a connection to church attendance for some, and for many others it absolutely did not.

While this type of spiritual interest isn't directly related to Christianity or the Bible, you can see by the statistics introduced in this book that there is a significant openness to discussing Christian principles and/or talking with someone who is a Christian about their faith. This data is both promising and important when we evaluate our ability to disciple young believers and evangelize the younger unchurched.

If this generation is wrestling with matters like faith and spirituality, we must be prepared and equipped to foster their exploration and even provide direction and guidance when possible. A church's ability to understand this need is essential. More urgently, their ability to capitalize on the opportunities that exist with this "seeking generation" will greatly impact their success (or existence) in the days ahead. We must understand and model spiritual depth, provide opportunities for others to grow in it, and establish churches that celebrate it.

It may be difficult for many Christians to see the current emphasis on non-Christian spirituality as an opportunity, but Paul emphasized that very thing, noting with enthusiasm that the Athenian philosophers were "already very religious," which he obviously considered an opening. The question, then, is what sort of depth embraces this element of mystery while emphasizing the unchanging, bedrock truths of the Word of God?

Implications (What Should We Do?)

Church Sitcoms

Do you like sitcoms? Do you know every episode of *Seinfeld*? Do you know the last name of all the characters from *Friends*? Can you still sing the theme song from *Cheers*? Have you identified people from your workplace with characters from *The Office*? If so, not only do you like sitcoms, but you also know them. You know how they work. There is a pattern. There's some humor, a good story here and there, a minor conflict, and some kind of happy conclusion that wraps it all up. Sitcoms are not meant to be introspective or introduce new concepts that improve the world. They are thirty minutes of fun.

That model is what many emerging generations perceive they experience every Sunday morning in church. A sermon is presented with a clever story or two, a problem is introduced and then neatly resolved in a thirty-minute time span. The result is that twenty- and thirty-somethings are leaving many such churches because they know that life is simply not that easy. They want more.

The first step to bringing in a new kind of content is the realization that sitcom-style church simply does not connect with an emerging generation. Sitcom content makes the assumption that things can be resolved at the end of church. It seeks to leave an audience with some key, practical steps to having their best life now.

Unfortunately content of that nature does nothing to embrace the mysterious nature of either God or life. Life is not a sitcom, and the real problems people experience involve deep struggle and introspection. Therefore, content like this isn't an expression of what true faith in the real world looks like. Life isn't that clean and all of its challenges certainly can't be resolved in thirty minutes or less.

Sitcom content often has a good intent. But most content like that is based on the idea that good teaching can't simply introduce a problem without providing sound solutions for life application. Whether right or wrong, most young adults see this type of content as lacking *depth*.

Depth

Depth. Everyone wants it, but it's hard to pin down exactly what it means. Should we use more Greek and Hebrew words? Does it mean exclusively expository preaching? Does it mean the elimination of illustrative stories that aren't deep enough? Or maybe it means that we do an eighteen-week series on predestination and thoroughly examine each word of Romans 9.

Depth is about the level of content. It's about engaging people at every level—emotionally, intellectually, spiritually, and even physically.

Though it includes preaching, it is more than that. It is about spiritual-ity as a whole, taking people to a place where every part of who they are is connected with Jesus. Worship must be emotionally and intellectu-ally challenging and so must teaching. In a sense, church should be the most challenging hour of the week rather than a sitcom where you can guess the ending before it even starts.

The depth of content is, in large part, determined by the level of preparation for a worship or teaching experience. In order to truly have this kind of depth, churches must be prepared for their time together, and cooperative sacrifice is necessary.

The sad fact is that pastors and teachers often get distracted from good preparation. The result is ill-prepared messages, ones in which the teacher has not had the time or taken the time to ask the difficult questions of a text. How can they be expected to bring something of quality to the table when there are so many other responsibilities vying for their attention? Moreover, some speakers think they have to be too clever or cute with Scripture, instead of just wrestling with the text in relationship to real life.

Some churches have recognized these issues and redefined their staff structure accordingly. Increasingly you won't find a "senior pastor" on the staff Internet page; instead, you find an "equipping pastor," a "community life pastor," and a "teaching pastor." This is a good thing, for it enables people to have a rifle-like focus on their role rather than a shotgun approach to ministry. The teaching pastor can spend twenty hours a week in preparation while not having to prepare the notes for the business meeting or do other administrative essentials of church life.

Pastors reaching young adults increasingly recognize the need to move more toward content. In a recent conversation with Craig Groeschel, a well-known pastor with a ministry that reaches many unchurched seekers. I asked him how his preaching has changed and he indicated that he has taken it deeper to reach seekers and teach believers alike.

Struggle

But depth of content is not just about *what you say*. It's about *you as a teacher*. One of the reasons why young adults think of church in a sitcom-like way is because they see very little authentic struggle from their leadership.

Think about it—a pastor stands and presents biblical truth in a way that implies that the pastor already has it all figured out. He relates no doubt, no struggle, and no experiential element. Depth is not just about the level of intellectual content though; it's also about the level at which the teacher has encountered that content. Depth requires that teachers demonstrate some genuine vulnerability, which requires some genuine "wrestling with" God's content connected to real life.

I preach just about every week to a church of three thousand people. Most of them will never have the opportunity to interact with me during the week. However, in my hours of study, do I wrestle with how that particular passage applies to me? Do I wonder at and wander through my own failings and insecurities? Do I really figure it out? Am I willing to share my struggles in such a public setting? If so, they meet me in the struggle.

A big part of transparency is not just the struggle during preparation of content, but the presentation of that struggle itself. A pastor or teacher can go a long way in cultivating an atmosphere of depth, as well as authenticity and community, by simply acknowledging that he or she doesn't have it all figured out. By including not only the informative content but also the personal content, including questions and struggles, people have the sense that they are truly encountering something of quality—a moment of true, deep, and honest content. And that's what connects.

Even for Christians, depth isn't limited exclusively to pure Bible knowledge. It's about truly grappling with and striving to process information, decisions, and choices in a way that honors God. Depth means learning about God as you simultaneously learn more about yourself and this world. John Calvin once said, "Nearly all the wisdom we process, that is to say, true and sound wisdom, consists in two parts: the knowledge of God and of ourselves. But, while joined together by many bonds, which one precedes and brings forth the other is not easy to discern."[1]

Michael Kelley, author of the *Tough Sayings of Jesus*, provides some added insight to the demand for depth in this generation. He states, "We like things tough. At least we seem to, and maybe that's a mark of our generation. We want to live deeply, think deeply, experience deeply. And while that might mean a little something different to everybody, as a whole, it seems to mean that we want to engage the Bible and God at a level that moves well past the surface."[2]

Allow me to affirm Michael's thought by echoing the description that we provided earlier in the introduction of this part of the book.

I believe it accurately captures the heartbeat and voice of the young adults that we interviewed.

Young adults are looking for and striving toward truth. They care about who they are and what they're becoming. Ankle deep doesn't work for them. They'd rather be in over their heads as opposed to kicking around in the shallow end. They like to study the "hard-to-talk-about" topics. They love tough questions and despise pat answers. They like wrestling with truth and chewing on things around which they can barely wrap their minds. They believe in processing and also find that questions are sometimes better than answers.

Kelley continues to discuss the issue of depth and faith:

> And then there's this: Life with Jesus is abundant because it is life lived deeply. I think we all want that last one. We want to walk deeply with Jesus. That walk is deeply satisfying. It's deeply abundant. It's deeply mysterious in a very good way. The hard part about walking deeply with the Son of God (or so I've heard from those who do) is that it's also deeply uncomfortable.
>
> The road to a deep, authentic walk with Christ looks different for everyone, but I think most of those roads have similar landmarks. Many of them involve a season of extreme difficulty usually because of life circumstances. More of them involve a commitment to practicing the classic spiritual disciplines that position us to receive truth from the hand of God. And all of them require an ever-increasing commitment to faith and obedience.[3]

Depth is more than just knowing that you should or shouldn't do something. It's also about understanding the *why* behind it. Why does Scripture teach that? Why do I have such a difficult time with this? And what does that say about me?

A significant chasm exists between behaviorism and transformation. Transformation goes beyond external resolutions. It requires internal struggle. It requires mining truth down to its deepest core and allowing it to resonate within you.

This type of struggling moves us from information to exploration. It transports us beyond the realm of intellect and into the world of experience. This is healthy. Too many times we equate depth with possessing a lot of information. Rather, we should measure depth in relationship to how much we grapple with the information we have.

The Bedrock

As the body of Christ, we affirm the Bible as the bedrock of our faith and the plumb line for our interaction with this world. As stated previously, young adults are looking for truth. However, many of them don't know where to find it or what it looks like when they see it. We must never lose sight of what we can offer this generation—the truth that is found in the Word of God. This is where an abstract principle like content intersects with a concrete nonnegotiable.

We live among a generation of people, especially younger adults, who are desperately searching for something that lasts. And quite simply, this world has nothing to offer them. But God does. And, in turn, so do we. We have truth.

Scripture tells us, "The grass withers and the flower fades. But the word of the Lord remains forever" (1 Pet. 1:24–25 NLT). Our God and His Word are never-changing, yet, constantly relevant. This should have massive implications upon our approach to ministry. Otherwise, how do we ever maintain relevance in this day and age?

So many times we commit countless hours toward understanding pop culture or programming our services to accommodate the social climate of the day. This is not necessarily a bad thing. But let us remind ourselves of an important truth. Our ability to retrofit God and His Word into today's cultural context will not bring revival. Instead, the only hope that we have is that God not only understands today's culture and this generation, but He created it and knows every facet of its intricacy.

We won't catch God off guard. We won't surprise Him. He is the Alpha and Omega, the Beginning and the End. Yet, in full awareness of our cross-generational shortcomings, He still willingly sent His Son to provide atonement and redemption for His people. If it were not for the power of the gospel and its ability to pierce the darkness of any culture, our ministry efforts would be hopeless.

As you begin to think about engaging this world with depth, we also have been given the ultimate tool. God, through His Word, engages us intellectually, physically, emotionally, and spiritually. The Word of God is living and active; it's more than words on a page. God's Word will not return void or empty; it will make an impact. The Bible is the perfect response to a generation that is looking for more. Furthermore, young adults connect with something that moves beyond just remaining faithful to biblical content. The element of story is often the vehicle that best brings content to life for them.

The Bible as Story

Content is about story. Stories describe the content of our lives, and as we begin to see our lives as just one segment of a bigger story, we have the mysterious sense that we are connected to something larger than we are. For that reason, in young adult circles, stories are incredibly important.

Emerging generations value the power of story, often preferring the Gospels to the Epistles. These younger groups appreciate that Jesus' life was not just an essay, a doctrine, or a sermon but, moreover, a story. Eugene Peterson observes:

> We live in an age when story has been pushed from its biblical front-line prominence to a bench on the sidelines, condescended to as "illustration" or "testimony" or "inspiration." Both inside and outside the church, we prefer information over story. We typically gather impersonal (pretentiously called "scientific" or "theological") information, whether doctrinal or philosophical or historical, in order to take things into our own hands and take charge of how we will live our lives.[4]

Early church preaching was often story-focused. A return to narrative preaching is a good thing—as long as the focal narrative is the narrative of Scripture. Jesus frequently used narratives in His preaching. Often the story was the point.

But we're told by some to preach the Word, and telling meaningful stories, even if they are soundly based in biblical truth, doesn't count. Preaching must be both narrative and biblical. To some, narrative preaching is telling a contemporary story with biblical texts sprinkled in. This is not enough. New Testament churches need to be biblical and present the whole of Scripture as their text and focus.

Fortunately every text has always been, in reality, at its basis a story. Paul wrote to Corinth for a reason. John wrote Revelation because of an experience he had. The Psalms were generated because of events in the lives of the authors.

We must not only connect to the words of Scripture but also the story behind the words. In this way, we can become emotionally and intellectually involved in the Bible, understand it in a greater way, and achieve a greater level of intimacy with the God behind the words.

Addressing Our Depth Issues Related to Teaching

A commitment to in-depth Bible study is noticeably absent in too many churches today. Some pastors and Bible teachers have fallen into the trap of taking the great depths of the Word, packaging it in shallow sermons and lessons that avoid the difficult or controversial issues, and highlighting only the major themes. Consequently, many of the people in our churches can't clearly explain major theological doctrines, let alone the basics of the gospel.

In a spirit of optimism and possible naiveté, I believe that very few pastors or Bible teachers set out to provide shallow teaching. I would imagine that even fewer desire to develop biblically ignorant Christ followers, and even less deliberately set out to disseminate false teaching. However, it's still happening. My hunch is that these things don't happen because of bad motives but, rather, are a result of weak and inadequate preparation. If this is the case, we must look long and hard at our approach to studying His Word and evaluate our need to change in this area.

Each of us has a unique approach to learning and teaching the Bible. That's completely acceptable. God made us different, and thus, we have various quirks related to the way we interact with Scripture. No matter what your style is, I affirm you if you are studying the Word deeply and seeking to effectively communicate it to others.

For many contemporary churches, this change has been a challenge. Much of the common wisdom about teaching and preaching was "make it simple," "make the application your points," and "make it easy to apply." I am not necessarily saying these are bad things, but I am saying that many young adults are finding this type of communication less helpful than their baby-boomer counterparts. Many who taught this simple approach because they wanted to reach people, are finding that they need to change their approach in order to reach emerging generations.

So, how do you get there? Let us make some suggestions. We all need some type of personal, intentional process that will help direct our times of study.

If you don't have an existing plan for Bible study and teaching preparation, then I would recommend something similar to the one below. However, if you already have a practice in place, make sure the following elements are involved. If they are missing, immediately begin to work them into your future process of study.

1. Pray.
2. Read the passage multiple times.
3. After reading the passage, write down any questions you might have regarding key words, unique phrases, historical background, etc.
4. Utilize available "study tools" to work through these questions (i.e., commentaries, Bible dictionaries, etc.).
5. Spend a significant amount of time evaluating how the passage impacts and applies to you personally.
6. Define the key point of the passage.
7. Develop an outline.

As you can see, this certainly isn't a complex process, nor is it a formal one. It's not supposed to be. That's not its purpose. You can add layers of details and personal technique on your own. But even these simple steps are positioning you to experience depth in the Word and share it effectively with others.

For some, another challenge may be finding the motivation to engage the Scriptures in a more profound way. Let us make one more suggestion. Find a group of pastors or bring a team of people together from your church. Then work through the above process together in order to prepare more effectively. Wrestle with these principles in community with others.

Cultivating Depth in the Church

Ralph Waldo Emerson said, "It is not length of life, but depth of life."[5] Interestingly enough, our research shows that young adults agree. As seen in the research, they show a high level of interest in theology, apologetics, worldview, and other religions. Many inaccurate stereotypes abound regarding this generation. Unfortunately one of them is related to the idea of depth.

Sadly many people have identified this generation as disinterested in a deeper approach to life. This couldn't be further from the truth. Those who have differing beliefs from ours are commonly tagged as ignorant. Those who don't act the same way that we do are frequently branded as irresponsible. And those in the church who are looking to reevaluate methodology are commonly accused of discarding solid doctrine.

Many churches have chosen to lessen their emphasis on depth in order to compliment their inaccurate stereotypes of this generation.

This isn't working now, and it certainly won't in the future. In fact, most young adults are turned off by shallowness and are beginning to walk away from environments (including churches) that foster it.

So where does that leave us? In essence, our churches must begin making intentional strides toward establishing depth as a central component of their existence. Here are a few practical "take-aways" that will help cultivate depth in your ministry. Take some time to process what implementing these would look like in your ministry context.

- Teach the entire Bible, even the difficult sections.
- Foster discussion in Bible study and teaching.
- Address tough topics and answer difficult questions.
- Do not be afraid to say, "I don't know!"
- Empower everyone to look for answers.
- Place a priority on Scripture memorization.
- Distribute the responsibility of spiritual growth to both leaders and learners.
- Provide opportunities to learn about worldview and other religions.
- Make apologetics a priority.
- Provide exegetical Bible teaching.
- Sing theologically sound music.
- Promote life application to Scripture.
- Establish climates of honesty and openness.
- Provide multiple Bible study options per week.
- Encourage examination.
- Pray.

Today's young adults may be the most intelligent, yet cynical and overly marketed generation in history. As a by-product of this situation, they accept little at face value. They ask tough questions and expect challenging answers. Thus, a superficial exploration of God, truth, and life will not be successful.

Our friend Margaret Feinberg agrees. Feinberg, an author and expert on reaching this generation, says the following:

> I'm part of a generation that longs for more—more of God,
> His Word and His presence in my life. We desire biblical
> depth because we want the truth of God alive not just in
> our minds but in our hearts. Like a diamond, we want to see
> the beauty reflected in a different shade of light so that once

again we find ourselves standing in awe. This naturally places a greater burden on Bible teachers to go deep and understand the scriptures and explore the context in which they were written.[6]

As the church, we have to be willing to commit to depth and stick with it. Is your church willing to make this commitment? Are you willing to go beyond the surface and challenge your people to do the same? Are your teachers committed to studying the Bible and empowering others to do the same? If your answers to these questions are yes, then your church is ready to engage this generation. If not, it's time to start making changes. It's time to go deep. It's time to stop swerving and side-stepping. Instead it's time to face this generation, teach the Bible, answer their questions, and foster discovery.

— A LOST AND FOUND STORY CONTINUED —

At one point during the band's set, the house lights came up during a cover of the old Romantics song, "That's What I Like about You." It was at that point Mitch realized how crammed full the Cozy Note was, and thought, Guess nobody here is the fire marshal.

The band was two songs from the end of its first set when Mitch saw Jacob break from the shadows and mouth "Sorry."

"Sorry?" Mitch thought. "I'm surprised to see you at all!"

Mitch smiled and nudged his head to the left in the direction of Ally. He knew if Jacob didn't have a great reason for being this late, Ally was really going to yank his chain.

He couldn't believe Jacob came. Of the four friends he either shared the stage with or who sat at the table in front of him, Jacob had offered the biggest challenge. He wasn't always the easiest guy to like, let alone try to love. It was like he was always trying to catch Mitch with his guard down, or challenge Mitch's Christianity. Mitch often felt pressured to be perfect, like if he slipped up it would validate everything negative Jacob said about God, the church, Christians—everything about which Mitch was trying to get Jacob to change his opinions. Even at that memory Mitch was thankful for Jacob.

James Cleveland for years had been the guitar player in the praise band where Mitch went to church. Ten years ago when Mitch's family started attending, James's playing had mesmerized the teenager. Mitch started taking guitar lessons from James soon after through the church's music education program. Mitch practiced intensely. James was a much in-demand studio player, and he rewarded Mitch's hard work by taking him to sessions when he had the chance. Mitch couldn't exactly remember when guitar lessons ended and life mentorship started, but he didn't know what he would have done without James, especially after meeting Jacob. Throughout college the two still met often at the Starbucks near campus for a brief Bible study, but Mitch thinks it was the chance to pepper James with questions about the Bible, life, God, the Christian life—everything—that had the lasting impact.

One of the lasting impressions Mitch had of James was the way he connected with people. He didn't just show up, do his thing, then scurry out of a studio. He knew people intimately. He knew about their families, their struggles, their joys. Mitch remembered sitting at a control board with an old engineer who was waiting on James to sit down so they could get started.

"This could take forever," he said looking over his half-glasses and through the window into the studio.

"Why's that?" Mitch asked.

"The drummer's mother just found out she has cancer. James is pumping him for details and he'll get them. I've been working with this guy for years and anybody who knows him knows he cares a heck of a lot more for people than he does music. He'd do anything for anybody."

That stuck with Mitch, and a couple weeks later he asked James about it. James leaned forward and put his Starbucks cup on the small round table in front of him. He looked Mitch square in the eyes.

"Listen Mitch, God has put you on earth for two reasons," James said. "To glorify Him and make His name known. You really don't have the luxury to dislike people. To dislike them means you are judging them. To judge them means you are forfeiting an opportunity to share the gospel with them. Not everybody is ready to hear it when you are ready to present it. Stay ready, and do whatever you have to do to help them get ready. Often that means dying to yourself so that you don't become an impediment to their openness to the gospel. Not everyone will accept it, but it is not for you to decide who gets to hear it. Love people because you truly love them, not because you are trying to notch souls on your belt."

As Mitch looked at the table where his friends sat, he remembered how hard James's words were to live out that first time he met Jacob. He'd been talking to Ally about a mission trip his church had recently taken to Uganda. Ally was interested because of her time serving with the Peace Corps in Ethiopia, but she couldn't understand how running around telling people about Jesus supposedly coming back to life was supposed to help people dropping dead from AIDS by the hundreds, and whose kids were malnourished and dying from dehydration related to malaria. At best she thought believing in Jesus would at least improve people's morale, but it didn't change their physical condition.

About that time Jacob blew through the doors of Starbucks. Ally introduced them, and Jacob seemingly lit into Mitch about all gods being the same and religion being responsible for the problems in the world. It totally staggered Mitch—"Well nice to meet you too," Mitch thought—but he quickly heard James's advice about aggressive people echoing in his head: "Listen very closely, don't get defensive, be humble, and challenge the claims they are making. Diffuse the emotion and get to the facts. They'll often see it is harder for them to defend their claims than it is for you to defend yours."

Mitch knew from Ally that Jacob fancied himself somewhat of an intellectual so he challenged him on that level. Admittedly he still takes pleasure in the look of stunned silence on Jacob's face after he admitted the church was responsible for a lot of the world's suffering and flat stated it was hypocritical for Christians to say one thing then do another.

That was four years ago. Mitch always left an open door for Jacob to walk out, especially after he and Ally broke up. But their conversations continued, either over coffee, through Facebook, instant messaging, texting, and an occasional phone call. They covered everything: existence of God, Jesus' claims of exclusivity, world religions, organized religion, moral and ethical issues. Name it and he and Jacob probably hashed it out. Sometimes the conversations got intense, but Mitch always made sure he picked at Jacob's arguments and not Jacob. There was once, maybe in a weak moment Mitch thought, that Jacob actually admitted if more Christians were like Mitch he probably wouldn't get so irritated by them. Mitch once invited Jacob to church, but quickly realized that was a closed door. If the conversation was to continue, it'd involve coffee or computers.

Now, Mitch thought, here was Jacob four years later coming to see his band. Jacob hadn't come to church or put his faith in Christ, but he hadn't told Mitch to take a hike either. His presence at the Cozy Note fired Mitch up. He smiled and thumped his bass a little harder.

"Now what am I going to do about Dean and his attitude toward the church?" Mitch thought.

Marker #3: Responsibility

INCREASINGLY PEOPLE WONDER WHY THE CHURCH, WHICH Jesus founded by healing the sick and preaching to the poor, is so uninvolved in caring for the sick and the poor. They are asking the question, why are the church and Christians not engaging in caring for the least among us?

Research (What Did We Learn?)

While the attractive graphics and Post-it illustrations in this section appear to neatly categorize all the data we acquired in our face-to-face interviews, it's important to note the fallacy of that perception. In truth, much of what we heard was difficult to attribute to just one topic or idea. Plus, our interviewees may or may not have been wonderfully articulate and completely capable of summarizing their thoughts into clear and concise statements. These people weren't worried about providing us with perfect quotes that could be later used in a book! They were asking why the church seems to be silent on many of the issues that plague their world.

A few years ago a series of tornados came through our community. Lives were lost, homes destroyed, and businesses ruined. As much as I look back at that with sadness, I also recall it with a weird sense of fondness. How could I feel this way when I drove through the community and saw the destruction? Simply because I say the body of Christ come together and act like it is supposed to. I saw it put down its' petty differences and selfish agendas and instead serve those in need. We not only reached out to the community, but we also became so much closer in the process. That's the deal with responsibility—it's a "both/and" not an "either/or." Responsibility, through service and social action, serves *and* unifies. In addition, responsibility provides a unique opportunity to reach the younger unchurched. Whether we're serving the unchurched or serving alongside them, our opportunity is still great.

In the interviews we sought to establish a level of authenticity, transparency, and rawness with those to whom we spoke. We needed to hear and understand what they were saying despite how they may have expressed it. Although it was important in some cases for us to "clean up" the manuscripts of our interviews for grammar and/or clarity, we went to great lengths to accurately reflect what we heard.

As you know, we illustrated the various thoughts and opinions of our interviewees by placing key statements and reflections onto individual Post-it notes. We stacked all the Post-its saying similar things into big piles and then selected one specific note to place on top that most accurately reflected that entire group of notes.

But we also had plenty of Post-its that didn't fit into a larger grouping of other notes but were still significant. These "stray" images both strengthened the significance of our larger findings and helped us form much of what we're presenting in the other sections of each chapter. You'll see how we've illustrated one larger stack of key images and its relationship to other independent "stray" images on the following page.

We also need to mention a quick word about the "What Stands Out" section. You'll notice a slightly different format in this chapter. This unique look is intended to show how several key images seemed to lack a real "take-away" until they were placed within the greater context of our imaging. Consequently you'll see that all of the "What

Stands Out" findings have been grouped together, with the exception of the one larger stack of images. Take a look at all of this and see what stands out to you. You may discover an added insight that we have not mentioned here.

Key Images

Key Image: Let's Make a Difference

- *"We have an obligation to know so much more than people did fifty years ago. Now, you don't have an excuse to not know what's going on."*
- *"If I say buy me five pairs of socks and bring them to the church on Sunday morning so we can give them to kids who don't have socks, they'll all come with a bag of socks."*
- *"I won't join your church if you don't promise to give me something to do in the first six months."*
- *"Service is quickly becoming an entry point into Christianity."*

— WHAT STANDS OUT —

- An increased awareness of societal needs and the impact of that awareness on young adult actions
- A desire for personalization when related to meeting the needs of others
- An increased commitment to serve in both the church and our communities
- An opportunity to engage the unchurched through many facets of social concern

Image: "Wow me, befriend me, and let's make a difference."

Image: "When I sit down in a class, I get out my laptop and my BlackBerry. I also have my iPod from where I walked to class listening to music."

Image: "We correspond through our blog as opposed to making twelve calls to see what's going on."

Image: "I'm hungry to be challenged."

Image: "What are you selling? I don't want to join a country club. I want to join Christianity, a movement that draws me in."

Image: "There's got to be more than this—something more than just my little world."

— WHAT STANDS OUT —
(INDIVIDUAL IMAGES WITHIN THIS CONTEXT)

- A connectivity to each other and the world through technology
- A heavy interest in technology and all that it exposes a person to
- A desire to be part of something bigger than themselves and what the world has to offer
- A longing toward a higher calling and personal responsibility
- A desire to impact the lives of other people in a positive manner
- A recognition of and an increased interest in the issues of the world

Statistics

As with each series of statistics provided, the need is always present to translate numerical data into quality analysis and practical "take-aways." However, it is never easy to clearly identify anyone's sentiments and boil them down into a few key numerical statistics, much less an entire generation. But, with the previous foundation of key images and the analysis and implications to come, this section will remain brief. In short, here's the number that stands out the most.

- 66 percent of churched young adults rated the opportunity to meet the needs of others (locally and globally) as extremely important in their lives, and 47 percent of unchurched young adults said the same.

Between this statistic and others, and what we heard in our interviews, the following conclusions can be formulated:

- Young adults desire to utilize their talents and abilities through a maximum number of opportunities to meet needs.
- Young adults will participate in hands-on outreach activities on a frequent basis that meet the needs of others.
- Young adults desire to determine their own beliefs through a maximum number of hands-on learning experiences.
- Young adults desire to benefit others through a maximum number of global service projects.

Analysis (What Does It Mean?)

Choices Make a Difference

What *is* the right thing to do? That's the question many young adults are asking themselves. What's more, they're asking it on many different levels: What's the right thing to do about recycling? Fair trade? Darfur? Or, what's the right way to invest my money? What about my time? Questions like this are a relatively new phenomenon, somewhat unique to this generation. True, people have always had similar concerns, but young adults are allowing these questions to change the way they shop, educate themselves, read, and even listen to music.

But the really hard questions hit even closer to home. What's our responsibility to each other? What does it look like for me to bear your burdens? Young adults have come to a place where all of these questions matter, but what matters most is how they respond.

It's a mystery to many young adults, both inside and outside of church life, why more Christians don't take their "responsibilities" more seriously. Young adults believe in global responsibility; they know their choices make a difference. And they are living their lives in a manner that reflects this belief. This was profoundly evident in our research.

Whether inside the church or outside the church, emerging generations are looking for opportunities to serve—increasingly, vigorously, and hands-on. Volunteerism is huge, as people want to make a difference in their communities and the world. Organizations such as Habitat for Humanity are seeing an increasing number of young adult volunteers.

Through all of these opportunities, both churched and unchurched younger adults desire to be a part of something bigger than themselves. Often they are looking to live life in a way that puts the needs of others and the environment before their own needs. They want their lives to have an impact—leaving this world better than they found it.

It seems we are constantly bombarded by opportunities to join a cause or an activist group. It's no secret that our society is captivated by the ideals of social action and global awareness. Today's generations have established these things to be of utmost importance.

Implications (What Should We Do?)

We believe that if the church is doing what is real, valuable, and making a difference in the world, young adults will give of themselves and their resources to support it. However, if the church is disconnected from the issues that plague our society, then younger adults and future generations will consider the church hypocritical, insignificant, and irrelevant.

Young adults already are actively involved in social responsibility, participating in both local and global causes. Their commitment to making a difference is resulting in an excessive amount of attention. They are highly marketed to and are in great demand. Political parties are investing great energy to recruit this generation, because they bring passion and activity to a candidate's campaign. Human welfare organizations are seeking after them because they have a responsive reputation, and businesses are trying to gain their loyalty. But what is the church doing to capitalize on this interest and connect with them? Are we reaching out to this generation with the same fervor of the secular world?

Churches can connect by offering an outlet for young adults' passion to serve. Genuine faith always expresses itself in ministry. As emerging generations observe that faith produces service, the validity of their faith is proved. We need to demonstrate our faith more by what we do, not just what we say.

The Impact of Increased Awareness

Why do young adults have such a keen interest in areas of social concern? What are the factors creating such concern and passion across our planet? If we can understand what's going on below the surface of this movement, we will position ourselves better to reach this generation that is so connected to social responsibility.

Part of the answer is simple. We live in a day and age when issues related to responsibility dominate the news. Disaster surrounds us in increasingly visible ways. Daily headlines, news stories, and blogs of earthquakes, tornadoes, and cyclones pervade the news coverage. The carnage is incredible. Although the impact of one-time disasters should never be questioned, we must be quick to remember the role that on-going crises have in our world. The issues of war, hunger, poverty, environmental decay, genocide, and illness run rampant.

Further, the advancement of media, technology, science, medicine, and more creates an increased exposure and awareness of matters that plague our world. This makes the younger generation distinctive. In the past, individuals were limited in how they learned about the major problems of their day. Information was harder to come by and could often be characterized as porous and dated.

This isn't to say that past generations were incompetent or incapable of effectively understanding an issue. Instead, it's simply an affirmation that it has become much easier for today's generations to access large volumes of information. This change has had a significant influence on the social responsibility movement. Quite simply, it's easier to become passionate about something when you are fully informed.

Young adults are the first generation to experience war in real time, visit foreign countries with regularity, and have wall-to-wall media access through the Internet and news coverage. These close-up views of events have greatly influenced their commitment to the world around them and heightened their awareness of social causes.

This level of accessibility brings with it an opportunity for personalization. As issues become personal to us, we are more likely to respond to them. This may be illustrated best by what's happening in the lives of young adults. They are a generation that has seen and heard many things, and they have responded.

Remembering Our Heritage

Now that we're beginning to understand the connection between these issues and younger adults, let's spend some time exploring how it relates to God and the church. This heartfelt interest in social action has taken hold of both the churched and unchurched. Furthermore, for Christ followers specifically, a unique obligation exists to respond to the needs of the world. However, this is not new to the body of Christ. Historically Christians have led the way in addressing many of the social issues that have troubled the world—abolition of slavery, equal rights, prison reform, medical care, and much more. Yet today some still believe that a disconnect remains between the church and social responsibility.

This is unfortunate but somewhat understandable. Although Christians are participating as much, if not more, than they ever have in the past, many others are just now getting involved. As general awareness and secular participation increases, the church is finding itself to be only one of many entities that are committed to the issues of our day.

However, it is extremely important that Christians be reminded of their strong heritage and unique role within this movement. It's easy to look at this rise of social responsibility and wonder how faith and the church can come alongside it. In response, we must remember that social responsibility is actually a foundational element of the Christian faith and a biblical function of the church. We don't have to wrestle with how we retrofit our faith into this movement. Instead, we recognize this movement is being propelled by many of the same principles and interests we cling to as Christ followers.

Let us not forget that Jesus was unapologetic about caring for people in need and called us to do the same. He showed compassion toward those in need, and He cared for the hurting. In addition, our God not only has an interest in humanity, but He created and sustains it.

As for the earth, the Lord breathed it into existence. Without His provision, none of it would exist—much less survive. And in the creation process, He clearly stated that both man and the earth were "good." Thus, at the very core of our Christian faith lies a deep-seated calling to engage many of today's social issues.

However, our opportunity as Christ followers goes far beyond any physical acts or humanitarian relief. We have something that not only addresses physical needs, but it addresses our spiritual and emotional needs as well. We have the written, spoken, and living gospel. Jesus Christ is the hope of the world! This is something we cannot lose sight of in our efforts regarding social responsibility. If it were not for His atoning work on the cross, this world would be empty and void of what so many are desperately seeking. Put simply, concepts of grace and mercy would be obsolete if it were not for our Savior who originally modeled them.

We shouldn't separate ourselves from the physical needs of our day—but we must always remember the spiritual. Jesus did. And young adults resonate with the biblical Jesus that announced His public ministry in Luke 4 by saying:

> The Spirit of the Lord is on Me, because He has anointed Me
> to preach good news to the poor. He has sent Me to proclaim
> freedom to the captives and recovery of sight to the blind,
> to set free the oppressed, to proclaim the year of the Lord's
> favor. (Luke 4:18–19 HCSB)

Simply put, Jesus came to serve the hurting . . . but that is not the whole story. The same Jesus who announced His public ministry in Luke 4, explained His purpose for coming in the Gospels of Mark and Luke:

> For even the Son of Man did not come to be served,
> but to serve, and to give His life—a ransom for many.
> (Mark 10:45 HCSB)

> For the Son of Man has come to seek and to save the lost.
> (Luke 19:10 HCSB)

The biblical Jesus came to save the lost. He came to serve and to save—and that is a Jesus that young (and old) can understand and follow. Let us be people that marry the message of the gospel with lives that engage this world and its issues. This is an accurate and complete picture of social action. You can't have real justice without Jesus.

Responsibility among Believers

The spectrum of social responsibility is ever growing. Causes and concerns are on the rise. Honestly it's pretty difficult to keep up with it all. Even if a Christ follower aims to maintain a high level of social responsibility in their lives, it's virtually impossible (and perhaps even irresponsible) to participate in everything that is in front of them. Nevertheless, the church can align itself in order to become more relevant to young adults in certain areas.

Serve One Another

In thinking about living responsibly, it's crucial that we address the immediate concerns that exist within the body of Christ. Hurt, need, and suffering are not limited to disaster-laden locations or to people who are hungry and homeless. Nor are they limited to the unchurched.

Tragedy and pain exist in the lives of all people, and it's more personal than just national and global happenings.

As Christ followers, we must be prepared and willing to provide physical, spiritual, and emotional comfort to one another in our times of trial. As seen in Scripture, this should be the very thing that defines and identifies us. John 13:34–35 says, "A new command I give you: Love one another. As I have loved you, so you must love one another. By this all men will know that you are my disciples, if you love one another."

Serve the Church

Christ followers should be serving the local church. After all, the church isn't a building or a physical structure; it's more than that. It is a growing body of believers joined together by a common desire to worship, study the Bible, and find community among each other. The younger generations often want to give more than lip service; they are interested in living out what the Bible teaches, not just knowing what it says.

Issues of doctrine and practice are certainly a part of the equation, but ultimately the church is about God and His people. And with this understanding, we are reminded of the urgency to serve His church with commitment and intentionality. Whether serving on staff, rocking babies, or directing traffic, the Christian's commitment to Christ's bride is commendable. While young adults are leaving some churches, encouraging signs reside in others. The trend seems to be that if a church presents young adults with involvement worth giving themselves to, then they will fully invest their lives.

Serve the Local Community

Opportunities for responsibility must extend beyond the walls of a church building. Young adults will serve in the church but not just for the purpose of a church getting bigger or more prestigious. It's imperative that churches begin partnering in other ways in the community to truly connect with young adults' desires to serve.

In most communities one can likely find a soup kitchen, a nursing home, or a mentoring program. These things, along with many others, provide opportunities for Christ followers to engage those who live near them with the love and hope that is found in Jesus. These touches make an impact on those we serve as well as those that observe it. When an individual begins to place the needs of others before themselves, it's noticeable.

Serve the World

The commitment of young adults toward social responsibility stretches far beyond local communities. The needs of the outside world are unique, and they often look quite different from what we're used to seeing in our own surroundings. But young adults aren't intimidated by their enormity, paralyzed by their complexity, or hindered by their locality. Instead, they are concerned with doing something—anything—and they make the proactive engagement of world issues a part of their daily lives.

The church can play a unique role in facilitating this effort, but it may take some painful reallocation of funding. A church willing to devote far more of their budget to mission work, both foreign and domestic, rather than their building program, will likely be a haven for young adults. Young adults focus on these kinds of issues when considering church membership, not the size of the building, but rather how global and informed the church community is.

Responsibility in Our Churches

As previously mentioned, this trend toward both local and global responsibility has significant implications for churches in a number of areas. One of the most surprising outcomes related to young adults' interest in social involvement comes in the area of evangelism. Service is rapidly becoming an effective way to reach young adults for Christ.

Young adults are being drawn to Christ and His people through social action. Among unchurched young adults, service (a tenet of responsibility) was cited as a major reason why they would consider (or not consider) being part of a church. Knowing this, we must focus our efforts toward establishing social action as a major element in the strategies and programs of our churches.

But this doesn't necessarily come easily, and it certainly doesn't happen overnight. It will require a shift in thinking for many churches. It may necessitate an overhaul of how we plan our programs, spend our money, and invest our time. This will look different for each church. However, all churches can take some key steps regarding responsibility that will better position them to reach the younger generations.

Teach It

The idea of engaging our world in a socially responsible and biblically driven manner must be rediscovered in our churches. As we discussed previously, the very nature of this movement is grounded in many of the beliefs that we hold dear as Christ followers. In this regard, it's important that we teach a biblical picture of what spiritual development and walking with the Lord looks like.

Some of our churches are teaching incorrectly with regard to what true spirituality is. We see this best revealed in faulty growth models that minimize or misplace service and missions. This came as a result of the previous generation's fear of promoting a "social gospel" that had no challenge to repent and turn to Christ. This overreaction by the previous generation is now seen as a glaring omission by this generation.

Too many churches function around a model that begins with worship, then moves on to fellowship, extends into discipleship, and eventually gets around to service and missions. Although these are foundational purposes, a problem exists with this model and its progression. It's not what we see in the Bible. The Bible never teaches such a clean, systematic approach.

From what can be seen in Scripture, those who followed Jesus immediately left behind many things and began doing the work of the One who had called them. They didn't wait to be taught and then go. Instead, they were taught as they went. This principle applies today with regard to responsibility, especially with young adults. Our churches must teach that service and missions are foundational to our faith from day one, as opposed to being the "bonus round" that we can access only after we've worked through the rest of the spiritual developmental checklist.

Model It

It's not difficult to round up interest toward social responsibility. It already exists. But each church is responsible for making itself a place where young adults can give of their time, their money, their talents, and their passions to something bigger than themselves. They need to see the church as a viable and relevant entity that will address the issues of our society. If this can be accomplished, then opportunities for evangelism and community impact increase greatly.

For young adults, loving one another is prominent. Serving the less fortunate looms large. Living in a way that accurately reflects the character of Jesus really stands out. Unfortunately an absence of these things stands out as well.

In one of our face-to-face interviews, we asked an unchurched young adult in New York City why she was not part of a church near her home. This was her answer:

This church across the street has been here sixteen years. In the whole time it has been here, I have never seen this church do anything to improve the community. The church hasn't tried to improve the poverty situation, hasn't tried to feed the hungry, and hasn't tried to make anything better in the world right next door to it. Why would I want to be a part of that church?

This question resonates loudly today. Churches that have abandoned the idea of social responsibility for the world around them are churches that have little hope of reaching or keeping younger adults. This generation wants to join a cause and a movement that is making an impact in the world.

Capitalize on It

As the emphasis of social responsibility increases among young adults, it will be crucial that the church learns to capitalize on the opportunities afforded them by this movement. Churches have an incredible opportunity to grow closer to one another through social responsibility.

Serving together unifies the body, potentially more than anything else. But, social responsibility is not only bringing unity to the body of Christ, it is also providing new and effective channels to engage the unchurched. While the unchurched have a reduced interest in traditional "front door" approaches, we should now consider using service as a primary entry point into the lives of nonbelievers.

Rather than initially inviting the unchurched to a traditional church program, perhaps we should ask them to help serve at a rescue mission or to attend a benefit dinner for a local charity. People are willing to respond this way. Meanwhile, the believers are getting to know these people and earning the right to share about their faith. Plus, this new level of relational equity increases the chances of the unchurched attending a small group Bible study or a worship service in the future.

This is a big shift in both evangelism strategy and service efforts from previous generations. In years past a church *served* those they wanted to reach. This is still an important and valid facet of ministry in the current cultural climate. However, one key difference surfaces with regard to emerging generations. Now the church has the opportunity of reaching people for Christ by allowing those people to serve with them.

This type of ministry and outreach is messy. When a lost person hits their thumb with a hammer on the Habitat For Humanity house, they aren't likely to shout out a "golly gee" or "Praise God." But that's OK. Our goal is not to condemn them; it is to build an intentional relationship with them. Through these relationships both parties are transformed, for the better. And just as serving alongside the lost is messy, so is serving them. But let us never lose sight of either's importance. At the end of the day, it seems we'd rather have messy relationships with lost people than not know them at all.

— A LOST AND FOUND STORY CONTINUED —

Mitch loved playing "That's What I Like about You." It always got the crowd fired up. As the song finished he flipped his pick in the direction of Ally, Dean, and Jacob. Splash! Right into Dean's martini glass! It couldn't have been a better shot if he'd walked down and dropped it in there. "Well, that's the end of that drink," Mitch thought. "No way Dean is going to drink that with the pick in it. Too much of a germaphobe."

Dean stood up, grabbed the glass, and chugged what was left of his drink, pick and all. He then turned to the crowd and revealed the pick clenched in his teeth and received a collective roar from the crowd. He loved it.

"I don't think that's his first drink," Mitch thought, "or he would have been at the bar asking for a replacement."

Mitch thought back to that first meeting with Dean two years ago. He'd been sitting at Starbucks with Ally having one of their deep life conversations when Dean walked in. They were headed to a new sushi place near campus, and he was there to pick her up.

"Oh good, I'm glad you got here a little early," Mitch remembered Ally saying. "You remember I told you about my friend Mitch. Well this is him. Mitch, this is my friend Dean I told you all about."

Mitch could tell Dean went into defense mode right away. He tried to hide it, but it was like every vein in his neck stuck out and his face immediately went flush red. The memory almost made Mitch crack up.

"He thought I was about to bring hell fire and damnation on him right there in the middle of Starbucks," Mitch remembered.

He could tell right away that Dean was wondering if Ally had told him as much about Dean as she had told Dean about Mitch. If so, Dean would know that Ally had mentioned his homosexuality to Mitch. And Mitch knew that Ally had told Dean that he was a Christian.

"Dean, it's great to meet you," Mitch said as he reached out his right hand and looked Dean square in the eyes. "Ally has told me so much about you." Mitch could tell right away that Dean relaxed.

Mitch personally believed homosexuality was a sin, but he didn't think it was any worse than any other sin that separated people from God. That was something else James told him during their guitar lesson/life mentoring sessions.

"You didn't do anything to deserve God's salvation," he remembered James telling him. "You may not be doing 'worse' things than other people as you judge them, but look at it from God's perspective. We've all sinned and fallen short of His glory. That means we are all in the same boat: people we look at who we'd call 'good,' murderers, people who cheat on their wives, people who cheat on their taxes, homosexuals . . . it doesn't really matter. When we look at it from God's perspective and truly look at it with His standard in mind, we're all walking in dangerous territory. If you're blessed to have received God's grace and know Jesus in a personal way, you need to see people as God does: in desperate need of a Savior. Are your actions toward that person going to push them away from the cross or draw them toward the cross? Mitch, don't pass judgment on people before you get a chance to know them. You have no idea what's going on in their world, and if you condemn them, you'll never get the chance."

Still Mitch wasn't real sure how he'd have reacted to Dean if he hadn't already known Dean was a homosexual. Loving people unconditionally may have come easy for James, but Mitch was still learning how to do that. He'd already been praying for Dean. The thing Mitch remembered most about Dean was how the two of them hit it off right away. Months and several cups of coffee passed. One day while sitting in their usual seats at Starbucks, Dean shifted uncomfortably in his seat and seemed preoccupied.

"What's wrong, Dean?" Mitch had asked. "You seem antsy about something."

Dean shot a glance to his left and right to make sure no one else could hear. He leaned in and with a whisper asked, "Do you know I'm gay?"

"What? Are you serious?" Mitch gasped, feigning shock and then cracked a smile. "Yeah, I knew that before I ever met you. Ally told me."

"Why haven't you ever brought it up?" Dean asked.

"If I had, do you think we'd be sitting here today?" Mitch asked in response.

"Probably not," Dean said.

"Why not?" Mitch asked.

"Because Ally had also told me you were a Christian and a conservative one at that. I expected you to respond like the people in the church I used to go to, and I would have been done with you the way I am done with them. I expected you to condemn me the way they did. Why didn't you?"

Mitch's heart broke as he looked at his friend. For the first time he really understood how hurt people are when Christians judge them instead of love them.

"Dean, you and I really aren't so different. You've talked about your dad not thinking much of you because you weren't a jock. My dad didn't pay a lot of attention to me either. He's a big deal corporate finance guy and never had a lot of time for us. Don't get me wrong. I think I'm brilliant," he said with a smirk and sarcasm, "but I think part of the reason I achieved so much going through high school is because I tried to get my dad's attention the way you said you tried to get yours. I couldn't figure out why he didn't want to spend time with me, and it seemed like it didn't matter what I accomplished, I still couldn't get his attention.

"As I started studying the Bible, one of the things I learned is that there is only one way to get God's validation and that is through Jesus becoming my personal Savior. It is His righteousness that God gives to me. Thank God for that because if I couldn't have done enough to please my dad, how in the world could I have done enough to please God? I don't agree with your homosexuality, but I also am not going to condemn you for it. That's not my place. My place is to love you unconditionally and be your friend. I want the best for you in every way possible. My hope is that one day we might be able to go beyond our general conversations about God and really study the Bible."

Mitch didn't know if Dean was going to hit him, scream at him, storm out, or start crying. Dean sat there with a dazed look on his face.

"I don't know what to say," Dean finally offered. "That's a lot. It's going to take me some time to process all that. You love me? No male has ever said that to me. God, how I wish my dad could have said that to me."

With that Dean was up and gone. Mitch remembers leaning back in his chair and whispering, "God, I hope I didn't just mess that up. Please help Dean think clearly about what he heard. Please give me another chance with him. Please help me focus on his greatest spiritual need and trust You to take care of the rest."

Obviously God answered that prayer, Mitch thought, as Dean dropped the pick on the tablecloth. Here it was two years later and Dean was still his friend. "Still trusting You to change his heart, God," Mitch said as they started their last song of the set. "And feel free to change Ally's too while You're at it."

Marker #4:
Cross-Generational
Connection

STEVE M., STEVE C., AND MARK T. ARE PROBABLY RANDOM names to you—names that are probably not important to you. But they are to me. They are mentors who invested in my life. They are all older men who invested in me as a youth or young adult.

I still remember Steve M. challenging me as a teenager. He asked if we could read Dietrich Boenhoffer's *The Cost of Discipleship* together. We did, and it changed my life. I did not have a license, so he drove my girlfriend (now wife) and me out on our first car date. At forty, he looked a little funny as a groomsman in my wedding filled with twenty-year-old friends, but I was glad he was there.

Steve C. met with me regularly in college. He taught me how to treat my fiancée, challenged me to deal with some areas of sin in my life, and pressed me to pursue a deeper relationship with Christ. Many times I did not want to listen, but it did not deter him. He invested in me, and it transformed my life.

Mark T. mentored me as a young professor. He was patient but unwavering—helping me to grow as a scholar, writer, and teacher—and I dedicated my first book to him.

I have since learned that mentoring relationships like these are all too uncommon. I have assumed it was normal to have men who would invest themselves in one's life and ministry. It seems that it is more unusual than I thought—the church today is increasingly divided by age. Cross-generational mentoring and relationship building are glaringly absent in today's church.

We are living in an interesting moment historically. Probably, for the first time in the history of the Christian church, generations do not worship together. It now appears normal that older generations meet together wearing suits and singing hymns, boomers wear Hawaiian shirts and sing peppy songs about how Jesus changed their lives, and emerging generations meet in dark rooms singing in minor keys. But, from a historical perspective, this is not normal. Beyond that, it is ultimately harmful to the church.

If we were talking about young adults ten years ago (which we should have been doing), it would have been acceptable to think of many young adults as those who were falling away from the church. And while a significant portion of today's young adults does fit into that category, there are many who don't. In truth, the reality is that many haven't fallen away because they were never connected to the church in the first place. And if this is true, it begs a natural question as it relates to the idea of connection. Who models a Christian walk to those who have never seen it before? This absence of mentorship impacts young adults as it relates to spiritual matters, but it also impacts them in the every day, practical matters of life.

I'll never forget a conversation I (Jason) had with a young lady about this topic. She said, "I'm twenty-four years old. I'd like to know how to cook, but I've never met my mother. Who can teach me?" As seen, this generation is looking to connect with those older than them.

Research (What Did We Learn?)

It's worth noting that much of our data and insights were separated into the divisions we're now using in this part of the book. We did this for our own internal benefit as well as to more effectively communicate what we've learned.

In addition, we must keep in mind that these different images are not self-contained or independent from each other. As a matter of fact, we saw significant amounts of overlap within our data. In many cases our statistics and key images have not only complimented each other, but they also have been somewhat challenging to separate into different streams of thought.

Distinguishing key thoughts and images is not inconceivable, but to disconnect them from one another completely wouldn't accurately describe what we saw in the research data. As a result, you will see what appear to be "repeat" key images in this chapter. Be reminded that we've shown these images again, not for repetition sake, but, rather, to magnify the correlation of it all. And while key images are displayed below, we've seen in past chapters (primarily from chapter 4) that new insights have been provided in the "What Stands Out" notes because these key images are evaluated within a new context.

Key Images

Key Image: Be My Guide

- *"I need advice from someone who has gone through the things I'm about to go through."*
- *"I'm looking to find a mentor."*
- *"Save me some headaches, some money, or whatever . . ."*

— WHAT STANDS OUT —

- A strong desire for relationships with people who are more experienced at life
- An increased interest in learning from other people's mistakes and experiences
- An awareness of both practical and spiritual needs

Key Image: We're Family

- *"I'm hungry to be known intimately and to be challenged."*
- *"I'll say liturgy all day if someone will understand my pain."*
- *"The greeter said, 'I don't know you' and gave her a hug. She just cried as she took her seat. It was the first hug she'd had in a year."*

— WHAT STANDS OUT —

- A desire for relationships that go beyond our own stages of life
- An interest in both equity and accountability in relationships
- A greater interest in relationships than church programs
- A general longing for older companionship and/or friendships
- A desire to process hurts or frustrations with others who may have already experienced what they're going through

Key Image: I'm All Alone in the Crowd

- *"We all have crazy schedules. When we do get together, it's a miracle."*
- *"Young adults are searching with an unsettled feeling, almost like a nomad."*
- *"Who am I going to call whenever I have an immediate need or who am I going to call whenever I want to go to Starbucks?"*

— WHAT STANDS OUT —

- An apparent desire for relationships that exemplify learning from others' wisdom and experiences
- A stage of exploration and discovering new things; a desire for a sense of home and being grounded; a willingness to explore new things in order to plant roots
- A desire for relationships that are intimate and authentic

Key Image: Help Me Find My Way

- *"There is a lot of pressure from our society about making money, providing for your family, and being able to afford a home and a certain lifestyle. I think all those internal pressures started to collide with me and they also collided with my faith."*
- *"Young adults are searching for truth that helps them live well on a daily basis."*
- *"I want to know who I am, but I'm not sure."*

— WHAT STANDS OUT —

- A strong desire to learn life skills along with spiritual disciplines
- A search for belonging within the greater context of other people
- A strong desire for stability in a world that seems to be counteracting it
- A search for mentors that model everyday living

Bring Us Together

Key Image: Be My Guide

Key Image: We're Family

Key Image: I'm All Alone in the Crowd

Key Image: Help Me Find My Way

Statistics

Although we capture the desire for mentoring through the key images section above, it is also important to recognize that our statistics from the polling research affirm what we were hearing. Here are a few numbers (we're really not trying to make your head spin with too many) related to intergenerational connections and mentoring:

- Forty-five percent of unchurched young adults identified the opportunity to receive advice from people with similar life experiences as very important.
- Sixty-eight percent of churched young adults identified the opportunity to receive advice from people with similar life experiences as very important.

After seeing the statistics above as well as hearing the overwhelming voice of young adults regarding this matter, we believe the following conclusions to be accurate:

- Both churched and unchurched young adults desire a maximum number of small group activities that promote relationship and belonging.
- Both churched and unchurched young adults desire a maximum number of opportunities to connect with a mentor.
- Both churched and unchurched young adults desire to participate in small group meetings to discuss life application of Scripture with a maximum frequency.
- Both churched and unchurched young adults desire to determine their own beliefs through a maximum of hands-on, practical learning experiences.
- Both churched and unchurched young adults desire information and advice from a maximum number of individuals who have that experience.

Analysis (What Does It Mean?)

As we continue to comprehend younger adults and what they're seeking, we must learn to appreciate the heavy value they place upon connecting with people who have more life experience than they do. Some would call this mentoring or cross-generational ministry. Regardless, the bottom line is that they want to learn from someone else's experiences.

Moreover, younger adults are looking for a connection with the church and a connection with people who are willing to walk alongside them and give advice here and there. They're looking for mentors who are willing to invest in their lives and teach them some things along the way. According to young adults, one thing that makes their life experiences more valuable is the opportunity to share those experiences with someone else.

Our research clearly shows that this is not simply an issue with those who do not attend church—both churched and unchurched young adults are looking for mentors and friends of all ages who have gone through the experiences that they are about to encounter. This is understandable considering the new facets of life that young adults are experiencing. They are starting careers, paying their own bills, beginning families, and developing new interests, just to name a few.

Some of these experiences are huge, life-changing experiences. And young adults prefer not to make the "rookie mistakes" if those missteps can be avoided. Despite any level of preparation or advance warning, they recognize that they'll still have some struggles. And that's fine. But, with a mentor, they have someone to experience the hard times with and also someone to rejoice with in times of success.

Though it may sound like young adults are only looking for what they can get out of relationships, quite the opposite appears to be true. Although they do cherish building relationships with those who are older and wiser than they are, young adults are also extraordinarily willing to invest themselves in the lives of those who are younger and have even less life experience than they do. These younger adults are committed to providing for others what they hope will be provided for them.

Implications (What Should We Do?)

Make a Decision

As we explore the ramifications of these findings over the next several pages, it's important to decide what we, the church, are going to do to meet this need of the younger generation. It's time for the DTR—*defining of the relationship*. Are we going to commit to this or not? What's going to happen in the future? What do we want to happen in the future? What will the connection be, if there is one, between younger adults and the church? For them, it's pretty clean cut. They desire to be in a relationship. Better yet, they desire to have multiple relationships.

The truth is that many young adults are willing to get involved in as many relationships as the church will offer. They'll volunteer; they'll go on mission trips; or they'll collect coloring books. Whatever the needs are, they are willing to step up. But they have needs, too.

Yes, younger adults will be happy to mentor a student or tutor a child. But they would also love it if somebody older and wiser would mentor them. They are interested in other generations, but they also want to be of interest to other generations. They'll use their talents, their gifts, and their skills. They're willing to invest, so willing that they run the risk of spreading themselves too thin. They're looking for a connection. They're ready to link up, lock arms, serve, and learn from somebody else. What if they could get that from those connected to Christ and the church?

The Biblical Model of Mentoring

Mentoring is a biblical idea. Although the word *mentor* itself is never used in Scripture, the principles we apply when using that terminology are found throughout the biblical text. We see numerous examples of mentoring relationships taking place throughout the Bible. In some cases, individuals were involved in multiple mentoring relationships. Sometimes mentoring happened on a one-to-one basis, and in other cases, mentoring happened in a group setting. However, the group was always small enough to listen to, and deal with, each individual. Jesus mentored twelve, sometimes three, and on rare occasions, one.

Moving beyond what mentoring looks like, it should be noted that Scripture continues to affirm both the need for and effectiveness of mentoring. According to biblical models, an individual should receive mentoring and provide it for others at the same time.

In some cases, the "sequence" of mentorship stretched across several generations. This connectivity allowed many different people to remain connected to a common belief, action, or cause.

Jesus' earthly ministry had a very distinct and clear component to it—*mentoring*. In Matthew 16:24 He says, "If anyone would come after me, he must deny himself and take up his cross and follow me." In this passage, He connects a believer's faith with submission to His leadership.

In other passages we also see how this affects a believer's relationship with the rest of the world. Jesus said in Matthew 28:19–20,

"Therefore go and make disciples of all nations, baptizing them in the name of the Father and of the Son and of the Holy Spirit, and teaching them to obey everything I have commanded you." This is mentoring at its best—walking with Christ and introducing others to Him along the way.

We also see that Paul, the apostle, believed in and executed a mentoring leadership model. In 1 Corinthians 11:1, he poignantly states, "Follow my example, as I follow the example of Christ." Wow. This is it—the heartbeat of mentoring. He continues on to say in Philippians 4:9, "Whatever you have learned or received or heard from me, or seen in me—put it into practice." In other words, he's establishing his life as one that can be modeled and looked upon as an example to follow.

But mentoring isn't limited to the person of Jesus or even apostles like Paul. We also see this modeled in the life of elders in the early church. Peter urges these leaders, "Be examples to the flock" (1 Pet. 5:3 NASB). Next, Paul says to the elders at Ephesus in Acts, "You know how I lived the whole time I was with you" (Acts 20:18) and "in everything I did I showed you that by this kind of hard work we must help the weak" (20:35). And though Paul is specifically addressing the need for responsibility to the afflicted in this passage, we also see a model of mentoring being clearly illustrated. In short, Paul is telling the elders, "I set an example for you, now you do the same for them."

These scriptural references aren't necessarily meant to show that young adults desire relationships of this nature because they want to follow the biblical model. However, emerging generations recognize that they have a lot to learn, and the Bible affirms a relationship model that can be used to meet that need. Moreover, because they live with such an experiential interest in life, that learning process is most effective walking side-by-side with someone, rather than just sitting in a classroom.

Furthermore, these younger adults revealed a special interest in two things that are related to mentoring and are worth examining.

A Connection to the Ancient

Within this younger generation, there is a significant interest in things that are old, even ancient. We see this in secular culture and also in the church. An appreciation for hymns and liturgy is resurging among younger adults and the churches that are reaching them. Things of substance and age are being embraced. This is also revealed in their feelings and opinions about church buildings and architecture.

A recent LifeWay Research survey illustrated this desire to connect with the ancient. By a nearly 2-to-1 ratio over any other option, unchurched Americans prefer church buildings that look more like medieval cathedrals than what most think of as more contemporary expressions.

When given an assortment of four photos of church exteriors and given one hundred "preference points" to allocate between them, the unchurched used an average of 47.7 points on the most traditional and Gothic options. The three other options ranged from an average of 18.5 points to 15.9 points.

This discovery is surprising to many. One might expect that they'd choose the more contemporary buildings, but they were clearly more drawn to the aesthetics of the Gothic building as opposed to the run-of-the-mill, modern church building.

Perhaps the unchurched prefer the more aesthetically pleasing look of the Gothic cathedral because it speaks of a connectedness to the past. Young unchurched people were particularly drawn to the Gothic look. Those between the ages of twenty-five and thirty-four used an average of 58.9 of their preference points on the more ornate church exterior. Those over the age of seventy only used an average of 32.9 of their one hundred preference points on that particular church exterior.

"I don't like modern churches, they seem cold," said one survey respondent who chose the Gothic design. "I like the smell of candles burning, stained-glass windows, [and] an intimacy that's transcendent."

If churches are looking to build and are trying to reach the unchurched, they should take into consideration this appreciation for the past.

We live in a time when technology changes so rapidly that as soon as a new piece of software is downloaded it can be outmoded. In addition, many younger adults live lives where nothing seems permanent, not even their parents' marriages. The result is a feeling of frustration and a desire to connect with something *substantial* . . . something *lasting* . . . something *stable* . . . something that has lived and survived through the ages. Perhaps in part, this is why so many young adults are finding a connection with liturgical elements in worship. This may also be part of the reason they are interested in mentoring and desire to be in intimate relationships with adults significantly older than they are.

A CONNECTION WITH STORY

Another reason why young adults are open toward older generations and mentoring is because today's young adults connect with stories. And most older adults have lots of stories to tell. Let's face it—the longer we live on this earth, the more stories we have to share. Stories of World War II, Jackie Robinson, bell-bottoms, and countless other facets of life captivate many in today's generation.

Story connects us with both history and people. Stories communicate important life lessons. These life lessons sometimes relate to things that young adults are currently experiencing or that they may never experience. Regardless, stories and the lessons they teach connect us all with the reality that we are part of the ongoing narrative of history.

Story goes beyond the accounts that we might actually hear from our grandparents, and it supersedes any one chronicle we can read about in a book. Strangely enough, the novelty of story is that it involves more than the tales themselves. Instead, it involves us in the process. It connects us with something greater than ourselves. As young adults look to connect with the past and with things that have more history than they do, we understand their desire to connect with those that can help provide it.

Establishing Mentoring in Our Churches

It's a struggle within the church to create a successful process for discipleship. We have created classes, lecture series, baseball diamonds, and countless other things designed to help people mature in their relationship with Christ. Many of those things have been successful, and a place can exist for them in the future. But some of the basic rationale needs to be examined in order to find the most effective means of discipleship for young adults. How do you develop a formulaic methodology for a generation that simply rejects formulas?

The answer is presenting itself, at least in part, thanks to the desire younger adults have to connect with people from a wide variety of ages. The discipleship that can emerge from these relationships reflects the way Christ discipled. Jesus communicated deep spiritual truth, but He did so by simply walking and talking.

Jesus' call to His disciples was, "Follow Me. Walk where I'm walking. Go where I'm going. And along the way, I've some things to teach you."

Jesus didn't necessarily seek out a fig tree, a field, or a farmer. He was walking by those things, and He used those moments that naturally occurred to teach spiritual truth. But He had to be walking with people in order to have that opportunity.

When people from an older generation invite young adults into their lives, they have that chance. Whether eating a meal, going to the movies, or having a conversation, the natural circumstances emerge to see and seize teaching opportunities through sharing life together. Though some specific direction can be emphasized in those relationships, the greatest learning moments will surface during everyday occurrences as they live life together—funerals, weddings, meals, baseball games, and family events. While mentoring does require time and vulnerability, the biggest key is intentionality. That's what Jesus demonstrated as He walked side by side with others.

Now, it's one thing to know you should do something. It's another to know how to do it. Fortunately the idea of intergenerational ministry is fairly easy to comprehend, but figuring out how to implement one in your church will require a bit more thought. It will look different for each church. However, some things can be done to help foster this connection between young adults and your church.

Do It Yourself

As with all things, it's important that we connect personal application to convictions. If an absence exists between what you say and what you do, young adults will quickly become disinterested. Thus, if you desire for your church to be a healthy body that raises the banner of intergenerational ministry, you need to personally be investing into this generation as well. Go ahead. Get started. Look to God for your motivation and to Scripture for your example.

Focus on Both the Spiritual and the Practical

As we strive to connect with young adults through mentoring relationships, it's important that we consider the spectrum of matters that young adults desire to engage. This provides the church with many potential connection points with young adults. Jim Johnston, director of Threads, uses the illustration of the Sherpas to help our understanding for both spiritual and practical mentoring.

Sherpas are natives of Nepal who have served as essential partners for the climbers of Mount Everest for nearly a century. They know where the dangerous crevasses lie. They know where to camp on the mountain for the night. They know when the storms are most likely to strike. Do you have seasoned Sherpas in your church that can guide young adults through the tough times in life? Do you have an intentional discipleship and mentoring process in your church where young adults can connect with older adults for friendship, help, and advice?

It's vital, because too many young adults today have no one to turn to when it comes to the tough questions of life (faith, marriage, life, and work) and also the practical questions of life (changing my oil, preparing my taxes, making my budget work, building a resume). Churches that attempt to separate generations drive cracks into the foundation of the body of Christ. But, churches that connect generations can be wonderful bodies of believers who respect each other in every facet of congregational life.[1]

Although you may not be leading someone to the peak of Mount Everest, you certainly can be a part of leading them closer to God. And in order to do so, you need to provide them with both spiritual and practical mentorship.

God isn't interested in being compartmentalized into certain parts of our life and not others. We shouldn't have a "church life" and a separate "personal life." God is pleased when we seek to live holy lives in our work, our play, our church attendance, etc. All of it should be worshipful, and God remains the same throughout all of it. As a result, our mentoring efforts should be ones that engage a person in all facets of life.

Never Underestimate the Power of Presence

The need for mentoring and having a connection between generations is personal. This isn't just another passing fad or church growth strategy. This is about real people who desperately need and often desire someone to walk through life with them. Simply put, this is about one generation proclaiming God's greatness to the next. Take Sam, Jason's mentor, for instance.[2]

Sam has certainly been incredibly influential in the lives of many young adults. Sam isn't seminary trained, nor does he have years of pastoral experience. As a matter of fact, Sam has sold insurance for years. He and his wife, Robyn, have two children, and they are a welcoming family that people just love being around.

Their home is always open to those outside of their family. Sometimes those visits are lighthearted and consist of just watching football games. But other times, the visits are much more serious— gut-wrenching, conversation-laden visits. Sam is always available to chat—quick to listen and slow to speak when someone comes to him in a time of need.

Sam has been known to begin mentoring relationships with young people and cultivate them for years. He takes the initiative in these relationships, picking up and shuttling young adults where they need to go. But he also takes the spiritual initiative, teaching the Bible and asking hard questions about their walk with Christ. Most young adults who have interacted with Sam would agree that their time with him has been foundational in their spiritual development.

But Sam goes beyond those meetings. He maintains relationships regardless of location. And over the years he has allowed those relationships to evolve into better and stronger friendships. He partners biblical advice with personal application, all the while keeping life's problems in perspective because of his own experiences.

Sam never set out to be this incredibly influential person. Rather, he just made the conscious choice to invest in others. He might not even characterize himself as a mentor but as someone who simply wanted to be in relationship with others. And perhaps, he even gets as much as he gives. Nevertheless, a lot of young adults are out there who are living more biblically, who know how to have a financial budget, and who function as mature members of the kingdom of God because of Sam.

Young adults are searching for truth that helps them live well on a daily basis and for mentors who will help them navigate life's experiences.

— THE LOST AND FOUND STORY CONTINUED —

Mitch loved it when they played "Le Freak." Sure it was a seventies funk song, and maybe the only person in the Cozy Note alive when the band Chic released it in 1978 was the Note's owner, Max Bergen. Aaron always got into the guitar groove, and the song gave Mitch a chance to kick the bass line . . . hard.

Mitch also knew Ally would totally be into the song. She used to call him Le Freak. The name stuck, at least in Ally's mind, after Mitch started tutoring her in a required statistics class. His offer to help her had been a lifesaver for someone who bombed her first quiz and had no chance of improving without help. She wound up with a "C" for the semester and as Ally saw it, Mitch bailed her out.

He shot Ally a glance as Aaron cranked up the guitar lick. She came out of her seat as everyone started to dance. He read her lips as she pointed to him with both hands: "Le Freak." He couldn't help but remember the first time she called him that. It was about three weeks into class and Ally was barely hanging on but improved considerably on her second quiz to a 68. Still failing, but getting better. The next week's score went to 79, and you'd have thought she'd won the lottery.

"You're a freak!" she shouted at Mitch in jubilation. "You're a math freak! Le Freak! Le Math Freak! That's it! You're the original Le Math Freak!"

Mitch actually kind of liked the name. He was kind of a math freak. He'd thought seriously about becoming an engineer but had a natural feel for stocks and market fluctuations so he opted for business and finance.

The summer before Mitch and Ally met, James, Mitch's guitar teacher and personal mentor, challenged Mitch to find ways to connect with unchurched people. "Look around you," James would say, "and pick anywhere to dive in. It's not like there is a shortage of people who need to experience the love of Christ and hear the gospel."

The week before classes began, James challenged Mitch to find one student whom he could minister to, and his task was to report the name back the following week. The challenge pushed Mitch beyond his comfort zone, but when he saw the look on Ally's face after that first quiz, it was like God was saying, "Well, here she is. I put her in the seat next to you. What are you going to do with the opportunity?"

Mitch was surprised at how naturally it all happened. Once he saw the despair on Ally's face, he really did want to help her. The thought of building bridges for the sake of sharing the gospel really didn't enter his mind at first. It was more like, "Wow, if this girl tanked this quiz, she is in for some serious rough water. She obviously didn't put much time into it. She'll learn, or she'll drop."

Then Ally told him how much she'd studied. Mitch felt like a real heel having passed judgment so quickly. He then remembered what James said about ministry opportunities and here it was. Before giving it much thought he heard his voice.

"I'll do it . . . tutor you. I swing by Starbucks and get coffee all the time. I could just change my coffee schedule and grab it when you get off. We could spend some time with stats."

Never in a million years would he have guessed that such a simple commitment would have opened the door to a much more complex challenge than simply teaching statistics. As Mitch spent time with Ally, he learned she certainly had her beliefs and opinions, and they couldn't be any further from his if he'd tried. Her mom and dad were into Zen Buddhism before their divorce when she was ten. Her mom didn't practice it so much after that, and Ally concluded there really was no point to religion. It was great if it helped people become better people, but she saw many who claimed to be religious living no differently than people who had no religion.

Mitch was shocked by some of the harsh comments she made toward Christianity and Christians. Finally he just made a stand.

"What's your beef with Christians?" He asked her directly. "You're relentless in your criticism."

"Well, first off it's pompous to think you have an exclusive God when all gods are the same, or that everything fits neatly into a one-size-fits-all theology," she said. "The leaders in the church are so busy dictating to others how they should live by some standard of absolutes, they conveniently forget to live by their own advice."

"Well, you are making some huge assumptions," Mitch replied. Ally was a bit startled at first by Mitch's directness. He wasn't impatient or combative, just firm and . . . confident. "First, I think a Hindu or a Muslim or a Jew would be offended that you've lumped their gods in with the same God I believe in. Secondly, it sounds to me like you have more trouble with the ideas of overarching absolutes because you want to do your own thing. You want total, autonomous freedom to live your life however you please without the threat of consequence. I agree there are too many hypocrites in the church, but that doesn't invalidate the claims of the Bible. Also by your very definite statement questioning the possibility of absolutes, you are imposing your own absolute by saying there are none. If you are going to require of me an explanation of why I believe there are absolutes, I am going to require the same of you as to why you don't think there are."

Mitch raised his cappuccino to his mouth and took a sip. He never took his eyes off hers. He could tell she was processing, looking for a comeback . . . long pause. Nothing.

"Let me think about that for a while," she said. She was truly stunned. First, she was surprised because he was right. She'd never really considered why she believed the way she did. Second, his honesty blew her away. Any other Christian she'd confronted got defensive and quickly fell into "personal experience" explanations, which she always thought sounded pretty hollow. "So why is your personal experience more valid than mine?" she'd ask. It was a conversation killer and she knew it.

Over time the conversations got deeper and the topics even broader. They talked about the abortion she'd had a year earlier and her former friend Ann's "Christian" response. Mitch shared with her his own personal struggles and where he had a hard time reconciling Scripture. In January of that following year Mitch's family got word that his little brother serving overseas in the army was killed by insurgents. It gutted Mitch. He wrestled with God over it and Ally had a front-row seat. It raised questions about heaven, hell, eternity, God's fairness, and God's sovereignty. James was a great spiritual support to Mitch, and it gave Mitch the encouragement to address those issues head on with Ally.

Ally has never put her faith in Christ, but she's also never stopped asking questions. Mitch once overheard her talking on the phone to Dean— before he and Dean actually met. "Dean, I think you'll really like him," she said. "He's real. He's certainly the most authentic Christian I've ever met. He actually has problems and admits to them."

Right now Mitch's greatest problem was going to be living with Aaron. That was truly his best set ever. He was raking the last chord, working the crowd into a frenzy before the big cymbal crash ending.

"The big question," Mitch thought waiting for the signal, "is why isn't Aaron a Christian?"

Part 2 Wrap-Up

OUR RESEARCH POINTED TO FOUR MARKERS OF YOUNG ADULT ministry.

1. **Community** is important to emerging generations. They believe that life is meant to be experienced together, and they sense a need to be involved in genuine relationships with others.

2. **Depth** is next—they strive to be people of deep significance. They do this because they care about who they are and what they're becoming—"ankle deep" doesn't seem to work for them. They told us they'd rather be "in over their heads" as opposed to kicking around in the shallow end. Young adults also expressed an interest in addressing the hard-to-talk-about topics. They appreciate tough questions and despise pat answers. Their responses indicate that they like wrestling with difficult things and chewing on challenging ideas.

3. **Responsibility** is a strong value because they know that their choices make a difference. Decisions are everywhere. Recycle. Buy or trade fair. Sponsor a child. Respect your elders. Tithe. Love your neighbors. Respond to the crisis in Darfur. These are the type of opportunities that define this generation.

They've concluded that all of these decisions matter, but what matters most is how they respond.

4. *Connection* is the final point of need. Some people might call this mentoring or intergenerational ministry. The bottom line is that they want to learn from those who have already experienced the things that they are about to engage.

PART 3

Reaching

IN THE FINAL PART OF THIS BOOK WE WILL LOOK AT SOME churches that are actually reaching younger adults. We created the criteria for church inclusion, surveyed (by mail or phone)almost two hundred churches to search for trends, and compiled a set of strategic ideas that others can consider implementing in their context.

We found a series of nine common characteristics in these churches that are reaching young adults.

Creating Deeper Community. Churches that are effective at attracting and developing young adults place a high value on moving people into a healthy small group system. Young adults are trying to connect and will make a lasting connection wherever they can find belonging.

Making a Difference through Service. Churches that are transforming young adults value leading people to serve through volunteerism. More than being pampered, young adults want to be a part of something bigger than themselves and are looking to be a part of an organization where they can make a difference through acts of service.

Experiencing Worship. Churches that are engaging young adults are providing worship environments that reflect their culture while also revering and revealing God. More than looking for a good performance, young adults desire to connect with a vertical experience of worship.

Conversing the Content. Churches that are led by authentic communicators are drawing young adults into the message. Though their styles vary from topical to exegetical, authentic communicators are true to their own personal style of communication and are usually more conversational than preachy.

Leveraging Technology. Churches that are reaching young adults are willing to communicate in a language of technology familiar to young adults. Young adults sense that these churches are welcoming churches that value and understand them, engaging them where they are.

Building Cross-Generational Relationships. Churches that are linking young adults with older, mature adults are challenging young adults to move on to maturity through friendship, wisdom, and support. Young adults are drawn to churches that believe in them enough to challenge them.

Moving toward Authenticity. Churches that are engaging young adults are reaching them not only by their excellence but by their honesty. Young adults are looking for and connecting to churches where they see leaders that are authentic, transparent, and on a learning journey.

Leading by Transparency. Churches that are influencing young adults highly value an incarnational approach to ministry and leadership. This incarnational approach doesn't require revealing one's personal sin list so much as it does require that those in leadership must be willing to express a personal sense of humanity and vulnerability.

Leading by Team. Increasingly churches reaching young adults seem to be taking a team approach to ministry. They see ministry not as a solo venture but as a team sport—and the broader participation it creates increases the impact of the ministry.

How Churches Are Creating Deeper Community

I DO A LOT OF CONFERENCES FOR YOUNG PASTORS. AND I AM guessing that for many of you, like me, you have felt a little "on the outside" rubbing elbows with a bunch of young leaders. Not because you obviously missed the memo about the current dress standard, stating all shirts must be black and untucked. Not because you were looked over during rush week by the fraternal order of the faux-hawk. And not because you were unclear whether this was a soul patch or a goatee type event. No—it goes much deeper than that.

You know the moment I'm talking about. There you are, messenger bag in tow, finding your spot in a break-out session. You've been looking forward to this session all day, hoping this will be the time you finally connect with like-minded leaders. You scan the room. Let's see, bald guys with soul patches, check. Guy with really funky bowling shoes that is trying too hard, check. Several guys that look like frat boys, check. Followed by the good hair, good skin, and sharp dresser guys, check, check, check. You try to remember what belt you have on and if it has enough metal without looking. In walk a couple of guys who either missed the memo or just didn't care, oh wait, they're the presenters.

Then it happens—everyone reaches for their laptops. You wince in dismay as everyone pulls out their MacBooks. NOOOO! You're the only one in the room with a PC (except for the guy with the bowling shoes who at least tried to be cool by putting a VW sticker on his cover). How could this happen? Wait a minute—Macs are what we used in school and everyone hated them. When did this fundamental shift take place?

OK, I'll admit it. I am a PC guy. Richie too. But Jason has a Mac. I always have been, and most likely, always will be a PC guy. I am not afraid to admit that I'm set in my ways. Maybe someday I will consider the *switch*, but until then I wave my two-button mouse in my hand held high and proudly pledge my allegiance to the always pending blue screen of death. All the while in the back of my mind I wonder: *What is it like in their world? Is life better?* You know what I'm talking about. You see them everyday. White ear buds, touch-screen phones, and seemingly unstrained backpack straps. The MacWorld. I feel like I'm missing something.

So what is it about *their* world that keeps me feeling like an outsider? What is it that draws them together, causes them to speak the same language, and gives them such a strong sense of loyalty?

Well. It's like a cult. EXACTLY!

In chapter 6 of their book *Built to Last*, Jim Collins and Jerry Porras write that successful companies are able to develop a "cult like culture." They say that visionary companies indoctrinate people, impose tightness of fit, and create a sense of belonging to something special with practical, concrete things like:

- internal "universities" and training centers
- exposure to pervasive mythology of "heroic deeds" and corporate exemplars
- unique language and terminology (sometimes secret)
- corporate songs, cheers, affirmations, pledges that reinforce psychological commitment
- awards, contests, and public recognition that reward those that display great effort consistent with the core ideology of the company
- celebrations that reinforce successes, belonging, value, and specialness[1]

So what is it about Apple that makes them so successful? Let's ask the man who knows: Guy Kawasaki.

Guy Kawasaki is a managing director of Garage Technology Ventures, an early-stage venture capital firm and a columnist for *Entrepreneur Magazine*. Previously he was an Apple Fellow at Apple Computer, Inc. Guy is the author of eight books including *The Art of the Start, Rules for Revolutionaries, How to Drive Your Competition Crazy, Selling the Dream,* and *The Macintosh Way.*

The Art of Creating a Community

Guy Kawasaki wrote on his blog on February 14, 2006, explaining how to create and foster community:

- **Create something worth building a community around**. This is a repeated theme in my writing: the key to evangelism, sales, demoing, and building a community is a great product. Frankly, if you create a great product, you may not be able to stop a community from forming even if you tried. By contrast, it's hard to build a community around mundane and mediocre crap no matter how hard you try.
- **Identify and recruit your thunderlizards—immediately!** Most companies are stupid: they go for months and then are surprised: "Never heard of them. You mean there are groups of people forming around our products?" If you have a great product, then pro-act: find the thunderlizards and ask them to build a community. (Indeed, if you cannot find self-appointed evangelists for your product, you may not have created a great product.) If it is a great product, however, just the act of asking these customers to help you is so astoundingly flattering that they'll help you.
- **Assign one person the task of building a community.** Sure, many employees would like to build a community, but who wakes up every day with this task at the top of her list of priorities?
- **Give people something concrete to chew on.** Communities can't just sit around composing love letters to your CEO about how great she is. This means your product has to be "customizable," "extensible," and "malleable."
- **Create an open system.** The point is that you need to provide people with the tools and information to tweak your product

whether it is Photoshop, an iPod, or a Harley-Davidson. Here's a nontech example: An open system school would enable parents to teach courses and provide a manual (SDK) for parents to understand how to do so.

- **Welcome criticism.** Most companies feel warm and fuzzy toward their communities as long as these communities toe the line by continuing to say nice things, buying their products, and never complaining. The minute that the community says anything negative, however, companies freak out and pull back their community efforts. This is a dumb thing to do. Indeed, the more a company welcomes—even celebrates criticism—the stronger its bonds to its community.

- **Foster discourse.** The definition of "discourse" is a verbal *exchange*. The key word here is "exchange." Any company that fosters community building should also participate in the exchange of ideas and opinions. At the basic level of community building, your Web site should provide a forum where customers can engage in discourse with one another as well as with the company's employees.

- **Publicize the existence of the community**. If you're going to all the trouble of catalyzing a community, don't hide it under a bushel.[2]

The list is fascinating and helpful. Much (though not all) of it is directly applicable to creating community in churches. So what are churches effective at reaching young adults doing to build community? The most common answer we heard was developing and nurturing a healthy small group system. Not that shocking, right?

"Life change happens in the context of community, and small groups are where community is really fostered" is a phrase that most pastors and leaders in the church world have heard. In fact, most have even recited it to their churches. Heard and said, but not always lived.

On the subject of how they create community, leader after leader expressed similar sentiment as my story above. One thing that stuck out to us was how many different types of small groups there were. For example, Steve Derdowski, senior pastor of Ambassador Church in Littleton, Colorado, said this:

We try to do a lot of different things together. We have small groups. That is probably the biggest way we try to build the sense of community. We try to get everybody plugged in.

So I would say about 90 percent of our people right now are plugged into different small groups.

So that's one way. Another way we try to do it is once-a-quarter kinds of group gatherings, where we get everybody together for a picnic or something like that. Once a month we have one big outreach, bringing everybody together. So we are building a sense of community while we serve as well.[3]

Later he went on to describe that his church has four different types of small groups. Sermon discussion groups (entry level), discipleship groups (for new believers), growth groups (for those more mature in their faith), and outreach groups (for those with a desire to use their gifts outside the church walls).

Much like at Steve's church, there are lots of churches with many types of small groups that do many different things, but all had community listed as their central focus for being together. In addition, we noticed a trend among the most effective churches, that small groups tend to be broken down even further by passions, affinity, location, culture, and heart language. Today's effective leaders are finding innovative ways to traverse the ever-changing cultural landscape—not bound by geography, demographics, or socio-economic status.

Some leaders are turning toward technology to help create and foster community. We will discuss it later, but here is a good question to get you thinking: Is it possible to have community with people you have never met or seen in person?

Some innovative leaders are experimenting with short-term small groups or *fast and friendly* groups. These groups usually run for ten to twelve weeks and at the end participants choose to stick together, or start a new group. It has the potential to be a great way to get people connected who are less likely to make a long-term commitment or are unable—like in the case of military personnel, frequent business travelers, or other transient types. I am sure some are wondering how much community can be developed in such a short amount of time. I would say depending on the context and the audience, ten weeks can seem like a lifetime. Ask a soldier about his or her best friend in boot camp.

Communication and Community

The majority of leaders we spoke with emphasize the necessity to keep talking about the value of community from the platform. Leaders said that without regular encouragement from those in a position of authority, community could become just another word used to market the church to the masses. Unless leaders are living it out and modeling community, they are unable to inspire others to do the same. (Remember the need for authenticity we discussed in the last chapter?) They need to be able to tell stories of how they are seeing people transformed in community and how it affects them as a friend. I am shocked by the number of pastors who say that community is the place where lives are transformed and that being plugged into a small group is what they want for every member of their church, yet they are not in one themselves. My Mac friends would say that is almost as bad as me knowing that Macs are better, faster, crash less, don't get viruses (unless they have an Intel chip), integrate programs better, yet still refusing to lay down my dependency on Windows. What sense does that make? It doesn't. Neither does preaching community and living an isolated life.

Another trend we noticed about communication dealt with the process of integrating the messages being communicated. More and more ministries are using small groups as the place where the pastor's messages are taken to heart, wrestled with, and applied to daily lives. Taking the message from the platform and chewing on it together in small groups is a great way to build a sense of community. Many churches are finding creative ways to prepare small group materials for their people that are a continuation of their message from the week before. This type of integration is not new but is being seen more and more among churches that specifically target younger adults.

In our research we did find that some churches reaching young adults were designing services specifically targeting young adults in their church. It is in those services that community is formed by a common language, style, and environment, while a sense of ownership is established. We are not referring to creating a contemporary service that is the same as the traditional service, just without the ties, and is led by a guy with a guitar. These services exist to help young adults figure out who they are in Christ and how He has wired them. A targeted service can help young adults discover what worship looks like in the context of their historical age and what style of teaching has the greatest impact on their unconnected friends. For the church this requires a tremendous amount of patience, grace, freedom, and trust. Trust that it may not look like anything you have seen before and that it may not be a bad thing. Mike Glenn, pastor of Brentwood Baptist Church outside of Nashville, in his insightful book on young adult ministry,

In Real Time, describes how his traditional church started a very effective ministry with younger adults through a separate service. His book is a great resource for leaders and churches desiring to create an effective young adult community and ministry.

We also asked Lee Rabe, pastor of Threads Church in Portage, Michigan, how they foster community since they never approach anything without community being in the mix. They refer to their small group environment as "community groups." With Bible study at its core, they constantly cultivate a sense of "living life together." It's not a sanitized religious gathering; it's pretty messy. Pausing for interaction throughout the teaching is encouraged because of the community it cultivates. They want to create a connective environment with truth at its core.

The pastor at New Song Community Church in Culver City, California, has a great plan for connecting visitors instantly to community. Each Sunday after every service, the pastor invites visitors to personally join him for what they call the ten-minute party. During this party he helps plug visitors into one of their small groups.

Several of the pastors we interviewed mentioned that meeting felt needs within a group context is one of the greatest ways to foster community. Isn't that what we all want? Spiritually—yes; by human nature—not really. What we really want is a group moved to compassionate action for us. We tend to look for people who will lay down their own schedules, plans, or agendas and reach out to us. True Christian community must begin with our own selfless love that emulates the dying love of Christ. He expressed love when He confronted Nicodemus, healed Bartimaeus, and died on the cross. We must deny our need to be constantly coddled and instead desire to serve as Christ did.

According to these effective pastors, small groups become a real community of faith when their focus is to go from words to actions. Incredible disciple-making takes place when they ask questions like, "How can we be the hands and feet of Christ to one another?"

Others choose to let community flow into a worship experience. Danny Parmelee of Epikos Church explains it this way:

> We have a large focus on small groups and as a church plant
> we started with small group multiplication before we even
> did corporate worship. So it's been part of our DNA from
> the beginning. One of my slogans is to "grow the church as

large as possible while staying as small as possible at the same time."

We don't . . . get caught up in that kind of false dichotomy . . . [that] large churches are better or only house churches are the real church . . . [We] try to combine both of those at the same time. We try to structure our small groups so they are intertwined with the larger corporate worship and all of the small group topics are directly connected to the sermon series.

The other thing which may seem kind of funny, but . . . for us food is just a really big thing. So the second Sunday of each month (which is when we celebrate communion) we try to do a communal meal . . . an altered potluck sort of thing.[4]

So what can you do? Well, this by no means is an exhaustive list, but it's a good place to start:

1. Recognize your need for community and get in one.
2. Teach the ideas of biblical friendship, hospitality, and interdependence.
3. Provide settings of small community where people can be honest and transparent.
4. If you are the pastor or a teacher, teach community AND DEMONSTRATE it with your message.
5. Recognize that community does not have to be a meeting; it occurs when people are friends and live life together.
6. Decide that your home is the greatest kingdom asset you own and should be used as a refuge for others.

That brings me back to the idea of Macs and PCs. I think the biggest hurdle for my making the big switch is the conformability and familiarity I have with the operating system. It has taken me all these years to be completely comfortable with the basic functions of a PC, enough to work seamlessly in different versions (95, 98, XP, and unfortunately Vista too). I know the core functions and I am content.

Meanwhile, only a short learning curve stands in my way of a great alternative to my mediocrity. There is a better answer to my computing needs, and I see it all the time. It is everywhere I go. I see it when I watch television. I see it on the street. I know there is something more, but I can't seem to make the switch.

Perhaps it will take a friend (or a corporate sponsor—wink, wink, nudge, nudge) who is willing to enter into it with me. To walk with me, answer my stupid questions, and let me know things are going to be OK, because as I hear regularly, "Once you go Mac, you never go back."

Once you have tasted community, real community, you can never settle for anything less.

9

How Churches Are Making a Difference through Service

EXTREME MAKEOVER, HOME EDITION DOESN'T HAVE ANYTHING on the all-volunteer Handyman Team of New Spring Community Church, Anderson, South Carolina. Don't get me wrong, I like to see Ty Pennington, megaphone in hand, yelling "Move that bus!" But let's face it, as passionate as he is about what he does, Ty gets paid big bucks for his home makeover show.

Though they don't have a Ty Pennington and they don't have the multimillion dollar backing of ABC or Disney, a band of regular "Joes" from Anderson, South Carolina, is making huge inroads into the pressing need for better housing among their county's poorest residents. Since its inception, the New Spring's Handyman Team has taken on home repair projects with passion and vigor.

Last year, after someone donated a lot and an older house to New Spring Church, the Handyman Team demolished the house and built a brand new home on the same lot. On Mother's Day this group of handy, compassionate men presented the new home to a single mom struggling to get a grip on life. They are so committed to the cause that they make it a yearly goal to build one home for someone in need.

Why Are Churches Seeking to Plug People in through Service?

Many churches treat opportunities like this as charity, seeking to fulfill a self-centered need to do good deeds for those who are "less fortunate than us." To the contrary, New Spring Church is one of a growing number of churches that have a vision for using volunteerism to transform lives. Not only are the lives of those ministered to changed, but also the lives of the volunteers are transformed as they serve. Today's young adults have a strong desire to change the world. They want to take an active role in making life better for others, whether that is through feeding the poor, digging wells in Africa, or decreasing their environmental footprint. More than ever before, young adults are thinking locally and globally about how they can make a lasting impact. Young adults want to be part of projects bigger than themselves, and they are looking to be part of organizations where they can make a difference through acts of service.

Kevin Marsico, of Northstar Community Church in Monrovia, Maryland, has his own ideas of why young adults want to serve. "I believe it's part of their spiritual development and how they honor God by serving the downcast. It is just part of what we are teaching them about relationships, connections, giving back, and reaching out to a world who desperately needs the love of God."[1]

Churches that are reaching young adults are successful in providing opportunities for service. We discovered many churches that purposefully seek to engage young adults in a variety of service projects and provide meaningful ministry options that make an impact like these:

- Mentoring foster kids
- After-school tutoring sessions
- Cleaning parks and painting schools
- Handyman teams
- Short-term mission trips—both domestic and international
- Volunteer teams for weekend services (i.e., host teams, parking teams, children's teams)
- Assisting with secular community events through volunteerism
- Backpack giveaways (stocked with essentials for back to school)
- Adoption of widows or the elderly

- Prison and halfway house ministries
- Hospice ministry

Obviously the unchurched world looks at life from a different viewpoint. This has always been true, and it will remain so this side of heaven. The unchurched person's motivation to serve does not come from the same source as a Christian, but churches can engage with the unchurched when it comes to meeting real needs and making a positive difference in the world. It may even lead to some gospel encounters and help build bridges into the lives of unchurched people.

From our research we were able to see a growing trend among churches. Many of them are seeking to be the hands and feet of Christ by serving their communities. Brad Edwards, pastor of adults at Cherry Hills Community Church in Highlands Ranch, Colorado, sees the impact of service this way:

> I think in reaching young adults, if you look at the demographic, the majority of them are very passionate about social justice and taking care of the poor. In the Bible James talks about taking care of the widows and the orphans, and so our strategy is once a month, instead of meeting formally at the church, we disperse into the greater Denver metro area to different ministry sights and we'll just go and serve together in smaller groups. I think that people who have grown up going to traditional evangelical churches see that there has been a heavy emphasis on converts and evangelism and not so much on justice and serving the poor. [But] it is easy to swing the pendulum too far, and lose sight of [the] true gospel, the saving relationship of Jesus and grace.
>
> I think young people are tired of not living out their faith, and so they are trying to find real ways to care for the poor because they see that as being essential to Jesus' teaching.[2]

How Are Churches Moving Their People from the Pews to the Streets?

At First Baptist Church of Cleveland, Tennessee, their aim is to make missions and strategic service accessible to the entire body of Christ. Like most of the churches we surveyed, First Baptist has experienced benefits from this approach both in the community and in the church.

Even with its traditional Sunday school structure, First Baptist of Cleveland doesn't allow its members to look at their church's four walls as a barrier for ministry. Each Sunday school class is encouraged and empowered to provide some type of service project for the community a minimum of two times per year. This process of moving small groups to engage in acts of service is a valuable way to help transfuse service into the DNA of a small group.

In our research small groups (Sunday school, home groups, etc.) are routinely cited as one of the greatest ways churches foster an environment of volunteerism and service, which is essential for young adults. Other ways that churches move people toward service are through new members' classes, Web sites, word of mouth, and weekend services.

Churches that are reaching young adults are encouraging their church members to serve more and more. Lee Powell, Senior Pastor of Cedar Creek Community Church in Perrysburg, Ohio, leads his church to serve by "lifting up the value of serving" and by honoring servants. Every week at Cedar Creek, a different servant is highlighted in their weekly newsletter. These people have caught the value of serving, as it is constantly brought before Cedar Creek's attendees through messages, publications, and servant stories.

In the past a person could not help in most local churches unless that person first joined the church as a member. The trend in many growing churches today is to give people an opportunity to serve before they join. At C3 Church in Clayton, North Carolina, Pastor Matt Fry has noticed that visitors are more likely to join a ministry team as a volunteer before they join a small group. Visitors at C3 Church, and other churches, see serving on a team as less intimidating than joining a small group. Many of those newcomers go on to join small groups after they have connected with others through volunteerism.

Are Young Adults Serving More than Boomers?

A large number of respondents to our survey revealed they are witnessing a greater growth and passion to serve among young adults, in comparison to the previous boomer generation. One reason for this is that young adults are acting out of a negative response to what they see as the rampant consumerism of the boomer generation.

A small number of the churches we surveyed believe that engaging young adults in service projects is a difficult task. Chad Lewis of Sojourn Community Church in Louisville, Kentucky, observes young adults serving every week in and through his church. As director of GroupLife at Sojourn, Lewis has a bird's-eye view of service in his church. He believes that it isn't natural for young adults to serve. Therefore Lewis says the church's leadership must continually model servanthood as a part of coaching their people to give of themselves through service ministries. Promoting true service to others must be to develop a lifestyle of serving.

Are Young Adults Too Busy to Serve?

Busy schedules are often cited as reasons that people aren't as involved in their communities as once was the case in America. When I lived on the north side of Atlanta, I had the joy of fighting some of the nation's worst traffic. With the continual growth of our nation's cities, my story is becoming more and more the norm. After fighting the commute home, many young adults spend the next three hours shuttling their kids back and forth to soccer, cheerleading, karate, football . . . you name it. With such hectic schedules, it may seem surprising that many churches are experiencing an increase in volunteerism.

In Bellevue, Nebraska, West Bellevue Church is making inroads into the young adult culture by engaging young adults in short-term service projects. West Bellevue's senior pastor, Steve Holdaway, is amazed at the service offered by his church's young adults, "We find that our young-marrieds—(many) with a couple of little kids—are extremely busy, but they have a heart for God, and they want to serve, and they will do something if you give them short-term projects."

Many churches in our study cited an increased willingness of young adults to volunteer for short-term projects that don't require lots of money, skills, or days/weeks away from their young families.

Catching the Vision for Your Church through Service

As we noted earlier, authenticity is a deeply held value among young adults. When young adults give themselves through service at West Bellevue, Holdaway believes those young adults come to realize that the church genuinely values authenticity as well. One of the greatest benefits for a church that moves its people to serve others is that their volunteers get a chance to witness firsthand the power of God in changing lives.

Let's assume for a moment that you have never fished. Maybe you even thought that fish came prepackaged and cleaned. If a friend were to invite you to sit and watch a fishing show with him, you might take them up on his offer (if he were a really good friend). In this situation my guess would be that most nonfishers would quickly become bored and lose any potential interest in fishing. If on the other hand, someone takes you fishing and you get to experience the thrill of reeling in a large fish after a great fight, then you will understand why others love to fish. You would probably even like the opportunity to go fishing again.

When we give people permission and empower them to serve, they will go out and serve. When they serve, young adults sense the greatness, the excitement, and the honor of being able to meet a real need for someone else. In addition, they will better understand their part in achieving the church's mission.

Why are churches promoting service to their members? Our research revealed the following reasons:

- Jesus modeled it and Jesus taught it
- To show the world that Christians care about them
- To strengthen community in small groups
- To gain an audience for sharing the gospel

In our research we detected a trend—churches were receiving multiple benefits from volunteer hours and monies spent in service ministry. Among these benefits were:

- Volunteers catch the vision for missions and recruit others to serve
- Volunteers come back committed to giving to missions
- Young adults sense the authenticity of the church's mission
- Young adults get excited about their church's impact
- Young adults invite unchurched friends to attend their church
- The unchurched community sees the church as an asset and a friend

This survey reaffirmed that people, who have connected with the missional heart of their church through service, can be some of the best spokespersons for their church. They have tasted; they have seen; they have served. Now they are not only inviting others within the organization to serve, but they also believe so strongly in what the church represents that they will faithfully invite their unchurched friends to join them. This, in turn, will expose more people to the gospel and assist the church in its overall mission of leading people to faith in Jesus Christ.

10

How Churches Are Leading Young Adults to Experience Worship

WOULD YOU CALL THIS A FORMULA FOR SUCCESS . . . FIFTEEN hundred members with only three hundred attending worship, all over the age of sixty . . . does this spell s-u-c-c-e-s-s? Though the naive optimist would say, "Well at least they are being faithful in ministering to their senior citizens," when compared to the younger, unchurched community surrounding them, it doesn't exactly sound like a formula for success. The new pastor, Dr. Mike Ladra, agreed.

After becoming the senior pastor (and I don't mean that as a pun) of First Presbyterian Church of Salinas, California, Ladra knew his new congregation would need to make major changes if it were to survive. A number of years later, First Presbyterian had tripled in size, averaging two thousand for worship with an average adult age that plummeted from a high between sixty and seventy down to a new average age in the thirties.

What turned this church away from a near-death experience to a lively church reaching out to young families and even the unchurched?

What was the catalyst for First Presbyterian's rapid change? How might these principles be applied to your church?

Though this chapter isn't intended as a course on resurrecting a church (you can see my book, *Comeback Churches*, at www.comeback churches.com for this), it is important for us to know how this change came about at First Presbyterian. In a nutshell the most significant change at First Presbyterian was the church's willingness to adopt a new vision for impacting their community. Previously with only a traditional worship service geared toward the older crowd, Ladra led his church to add a second worship service aimed to attract a younger crowd. Noticing more room to expand by reaching into an ever-increasing unchurched community, Ladra led First Presbyterian to add a third service with a more contemporary feel. This third service featured what Ladra called "U2 type music, (that is) very edgy . . . the kind of music that twenty-five and thirty-year-olds listen to on the radio."

First Presbyterian's newest service, added only eighteen months ago, took off immediately, and it has doubled in attendance during the past five months, attracting mostly young singles and young families. This success has spilled over into First Presbyterian's Sunday school, filling up their second Sunday school hour in just a few months.

Our research revealed that the vast majority of churches that are reaching young adults do so in a contemporary setting (either the main service or an additional worship time). Some churches have kept their traditional or contemporary services while adding new services similar to the third service at First Presbyterian. Of this type service, Ladra comments that the music is "way beyond contemporary." Additionally Ladra says:

> The other key element we added was the lights. We found
> that as we studied that age group [young adults], that they
> are attracted to a concert-like atmosphere. It is the very
> atmosphere that most churchgoing people—even those in
> their forties and fifties would criticize as not worshipful.
> I just think the reason that a lot of churches are not reaching
> the under-forty crowd, but especially the under-thirty crowd
> is music. And they are not willing to do the lighting effects—
> and it is far more important than I realized even five years
> ago.[1]

Dave Ferguson, lead pastor of Community Christian Church in Naperville, Illinois, has seen a similar trend in his ministry toward the effectiveness of a radically different way of worship for young adults. Asked about his church's services, Dave replied:

> I can tell you the first thing, from an outsider looking in, they would say it is very aggressive. It is very contemporary. I think we would probably describe it as more eclectic as far as stylistic. I mean you can come on one week and [then on the very next week] it is a little bit different. But for the most part you could show up one weekend and it could be full out rock and roll. The next week it might be a jazz band, an orchestra, or if you go another weekend, we [might] have a gospel choir.
>
> We have nine different locations. And so there is also some variation from site to site. We have a couple of different locations that are a lot more multicultural than others and so they tend to do a lot more of the gospel stuff in one location. Another one, it is in a community that is 95 percent Hispanic. So I'd say as a whole, though, all of our services are pretty eclectic.[2]

Those who have followed Dave Ferguson for long know that he is really into what he calls the "big idea." Even with the variety of people served by all of Community Christian's multiple campuses, Dave says his leadership gears their services around their one big idea. Expounding on their big idea, David says:

> We want everybody to leave with [knowing] how to put that into life and really live that out. We are pretty relentless about that. That comes through the teaching and it comes through the other experiential stuff that we do throughout the rest of the service and it is also the same big idea with our students, children, large groups, and our small groups.[3]

Describing the worship at C3 Church, Senior Pastor Matt Fry says, "Our worship is very passionate, very high energy, very engaging, and experiential." As mentioned earlier, a lot of older and traditionally churched people may feel such radical departures from the norm is entertainment, not church. Fry responds, "It is almost like a rock concert, but it's not entertainment mode. It is more participation mode."

To further define what he terms, "participation mode," Fry answered:

We want to create an environment where people can come and they can experience God, where they can experience His power and our services can tend to be, at times, a little bit emotional. From the very beginning of our church we wanted people to be able to experience God and not just come and listen to a sermon and listen to music and leave, but to actually touch, taste, experience, feel, and know that God is real.

We are not a spectator church, but we want people to participate and to experience God. I like to involve our people in the sermon, whether it is reading along or taking notes. Let's all be involved in this. This is not I'm up here talking and you're listening; and it is not that the band is up there [just] singing, but we want people to be involved and to participate.[4]

Styles of Music Used in Churches Reaching Young Adults

- Band
- Rock and roll
- Driven
- Modern
- Pop

In our research we found many churches that have moved to alternative styles of worship—some using the term "ancient future." It was common to find "contemporary" and "hymn" mentioned as a common approach rather than two different styles.

To be clear, we are not talking about visiting an uptown high-church where the music director waves his hand to conduct congregational singing. We're also not speaking of a southern country church where the music director calls out verse numbers between verses. Instead, these churches take a revamped approach to hymns. Usually these occasional hymns are done in either a very simple, guitar-driven format or full on with a revamped rock styling. Again, what we're seeing here is not so much a specific stylistic preference, but rather musical worship that is God-centered, biblically based, culturally appealing, and done with excellence.

Churches like Westside Church in Flushing, Wisconsin, beyond musical styles to help young people experience worship. Ed Emmerling explained it this way:

> We have done several participatory things, like we had an art wall during one service. We painted a backdrop behind our stage, just a plain color. And then we did a couple of weeks preaching on responding to God from within and then we gave people a chance to respond however God led them to—they could write a verse up there, they could draw a picture. They would write a prayer, a praise, whatever. I was also blown away at the response of people.[5]

Worship is always a flash point in churches—but churches that are reaching young adults have moved beyond the debates and into the mission. Most, though not all, are contemporary. Some are in a church with other more traditional services. Others are not. However, all find worship to be an essential part of engaging emerging generations.

How Churches Are
Delivering Content

ON JANUARY 10, 1984, WENDY'S BEGAN AN AD CAMPAIGN
featuring a couple of old ladies calling out, "Where's the beef?" We've
all ordered a burger before and wondered if the meat portion was getting smaller and smaller. These commercials indicated that Wendy's was
not going to skimp on the amount of beef in each burger, unlike their
competitors.

In some circles there's been a lot of talk about churches watering
down the message in order to attract more people. Frankly I believe
many large churches are unfairly labeled this way. I know many large
church pastors who faithfully teach God's Word week after week.

The point of our study wasn't to determine whether or not a church
was being faithful as a Bible-teaching church or who's watering down
the message and who's not.

Our purpose was to consider churches that are reaching young
adults: What is their teaching style, how do they deliver their content,
and do they believe they are being effective with their goals for content?
As a point of reference for this chapter, we will refer to the weekend
message as the content, though we are well aware it is not. The content
is what could be considered the meat.

The Content, the Message . . . That's the Point

I (Scott) have the privilege of serving on the faculty of Trinity Evangelical Divinity School and Southwestern Seminary. Anyone who has attended a chapel service at Southeastern in Wake Forest, North Carolina, for the last decade has probably heard Dr. Logan Carson, Distinguished Professor of Christian Theology. Dr. Carson is a humble servant who loves the Lord and the students God sends his way. A hallmark of the modern Southeastern, Dr. Carson helps ensure a lively chapel service. If Dr. Carson believes the visiting preacher or lecturer is doing a fine job in a message, he will often talk back to the speaker, "That's the point! Awe . . . yes! Preach it!" Dr. Carson knows a good message when he hears it. When you hear "Preach, preach, preach" and "That's the point," you know Southeastern's visiting chapel speaker has hit a chord with Carson.

The content is the point. Everything that's done on a Sunday—the greeting in the parking lot, the children's classes, the music, the videos, the drama—it is all done with the intention of leading up to the point of a solid, life-transforming message. The goal of focusing everything toward the message is to let the Word of God lead faithless people to faith and grow people in their faith.

Nowadays people are using many different labels for the content:

- preaching
- sermons
- messages
- talks

We also discovered a wide array of styles for content delivery. Church leaders revealed the following two primary styles:

- expository
- topical

In addition, another list of message styles emerged in our study: book studies, thematic, conversational, and narrative/storytelling. These styles are sometimes held as independent styles like expository and topical messages, but they could easily be woven into the fabric of expository or topical messages.

The greatest determining factor for how these would align as a version of either expository or topical teaching has to do with the development of the message. In other words, does the pastor do an expository message on Job by telling a story or does the pastor use Job's life story to develop a topic?

Our research reveals that many of these styles overlap with one another. For instance, some churches may do a book study that is more verse-by-verse and chapter-by-chapter, while some may do book studies that identify and study a book's major themes. One pastor may use storytelling to walk through parts of the Gospels, while another may use storytelling to do a more topical message. A thematic approach may be a verse-by-verse study of selected passages wrapped around a certain theme.

Typically most leaders of churches reaching young adults described their content delivery as either expository or topical. Some pastors weren't so concerned about the labeling. Others expressed sentiments revealing they have sensed undue judging by their peers. We discovered a larger number of topical preachers felt unfairly judged than expository preachers. Most likely the debate between the two camps will continue until Christ returns.

The Topical Approach

Marty Mosher of The Fellowship at Plum Creek in Kyle, Texas, describes his content delivery as "topical on a topic and verse with verse rather than verse-by-verse." In giving his reason for topical teaching, Marty commented:

> It is on topics in the Bible where the needs of believers and unbelievers overlap. Everybody that is a parent needs to be a better parent, so that is a need they have. But then there is a centrality of the cross and the gospel in every message no matter what the topic. In other words, for us the good news of Jesus is presented every single week, somehow woven into that sermon.[1]

Returning to his example on a topical sermon, Marty mentioned one simple way to present the gospel would be to add, "You know, we have told you how to be a good parent. Oh, by the way, you can't. You need Jesus." Such an approach would then open the door for a pastor to speak of Jesus, sin, repentance, and the promise of heaven. According to our research, this is a common way utilized by many churches to bridge the gospel to the lost using topical sermons.

Marty is among a number of those who once criticized topical teaching "as shallow and less than biblical." Another criticism faced by some leaders is that topical pastors are overly seeker sensitive to the point of allowing the truth of Scripture to be overpowered by the tide of popular opinion. While this may be true for some, Marty believes this isn't true for all. Take abortion for example. Marty has addressed the issue but likes to believe he has done so with gentleness and respect, purposely avoiding ridicule of those with opposing views.

Are Expository Messages on the Rebound?

Anyone watching the church world for the past few decades knows there has been a great migration of pastors toward topical sermons. One thing that has surprised us in our survey on content delivery is the vast number of churches reaching young adults through expository weekend messages. An expository message, in its purest sense, would be one that "exposes the text." It would begin with the text, define and explain the text, and help apply the text to life.

Lakeridge Church in Broomfield, Colorado, is like many churches that have intentionally positioned themselves to engage the culture with the gospel. In the past Lakeridge has unapologetically leaned heavily to a more topical message—focusing on current issues from pop culture.

When we asked Roger Whitmore, community care pastor at Lakeridge, if he believed young adults were more attracted to this topical style rather than verse by verse exposition, Whitmore surprised us saying, "I am definitely beginning to believe they do not." Whitmore explained that though he wasn't downing the topical approach, he did not believe it was "as important as we have deemed it to be."

Such a story line reminds us of a conversation that recently came out of the leaders from Willow Creek in Illinois. Though Bill Hybels and the leaders of Willow Creek did not discount their topical approach, they did express that they did not see quite the returns they had expected. All in all, the new understanding from Willow Creek's own self-assessment is that the leaders of the church need to regularly communicate to the people the personal responsibility each person has to get in God's Word for deeper study.

Speaking of the recent learning curve at Lakeridge Church, Whitmore elaborated, "You are talking to me at a time when we are struggling a little bit, where we really had a nice little growth curve and now it is plateaued, and, frankly, starting to decline a little bit, and folks are saying they want deeper teaching."

This craving for deeper teaching isn't limited to the fifty-plus crowd. Referring back to his church's situation, Whitmore said, "All those older ones have already gone." According to Whitmore, they have heard echos of a call for deeper truths from those in their twenties and thirties at Lakeridge Church and on college campuses where Whitmore says some campus leaders are "saying their students just want truth."

Why have some organizations begun backing away from a more seeker sensitive, pop-culture aware, topical-styled approach? Though this trend isn't replicated everywhere, it is a trend to watch—and one we heard mentioned frequently. It is easy to jump to conclusions and to declare this one situation is proof that the topical message doesn't work. It is probably a wiser thing to look at the total landscape that is out there and see which growth principles are universal. Looking across the entire landscape, we can still observe rapid growth in many seeker sensitive churches. We can also find many examples of rapidly growing churches using a more expository message model.

Can a Church Reach Young Adults with Expository Messages?

From our survey we learned that just over half of the churches effectively reaching young adults use a more expository teaching style. These are not necessarily churches that systematically walk through the Scriptures from cover to cover, but they do identify more with an expository approach than anything else.

Pastor to C3 Church in the Raleigh suburb of Clayton, North Carolina, Matt Fry talks about his own self-styled, expository messages:

> I am not a verse-by-verse kind of guy where I'll start in
> Genesis and go through Revelation, although we will take
> a book in the Bible and develop a series through a certain
> book. My preaching style is typically to take a passage of
> Scripture and develop my outline from that Scripture—letting
> the Scripture kind of drive the outline.[2]

But Matt doesn't buy the argument that expository messages are lifeless and distanced from real life. Like the millions who attend churches where expository messages are the norm, Matt believes, if done right, an expository message can indeed connect with the world of the unbelieving or unchurched. Listen to the way Matt describes his messages:

> It is going to be very, very Scripture driven [with a] high content of Scripture, and there is going to be some kind of challenge in there. We're going to come out of that [challenge] going, "OK, here's how you need to live this sermon out."[3]

Pastor to Next Generation Ministries at San Antonio's Community Bible Church, Scott Austin believes churches are beginning to experience a gradual shift in focus back to expository teaching. He says, "Even the younger groups of Christians are falling back to a more exegetical preaching and wanting more (of a) straight up, just open up the Bible and go through John or go through Ephesians" approach.

I asked Mark Driscoll, pastor of Mars Hill Church in Seattle, why he thinks text-driven preaching is making a comeback. He e-mailed:

> What I am seeing both around the nation and world is that younger preachers having the biggest crowds and most conversions are those who preach longer expositional sermons. While these younger preachers are not enslaved by expository preaching and do also preach topical series upon occasion, they are able to see books of the Bible as unified true stories and focus on the characters and narrative themes in such a way as to capture the hearts and minds of younger and more secular people. And their audiences tend to feel much safer staying in a book of the Bible and examining portions in the story line of the book as opposed to pulling verses from various books of the Bible into a systematic presentation. Subsequently this has also led to a growing desire for young preachers to preach through longer Old Testament narrative books which I believe is a good trend as all of God's Word is getting equal consideration.[4]

The result of our survey seems to indicate that people are not so much interested in the method of delivery as they are in the delivery of TRUTH that is relevant to their lives. Authentic preaching that presents God's Word as the answer will draw many people.

Mixing It Up, Expository and Topical

Danny Parmelee, senior pastor of Epikos Church in Milwaukee, Wisconsin, represents a growing number of pastors who intentionally vary between topical and expository teaching styles. Danny typically will teach through books of the Bible from fall through spring, while saving the summer for a topical study. Danny's style leans more to expository, but also shares common ingredients with topical teaching.

Senior pastor to Community Bible Church in the suburban Atlanta community of Stockbridge, Georgia, Beau Adams also generally uses a more topical approach to message preparation and delivery. Adams, however, doesn't feel bound by one style. Like many pastors, he uses a flex fuel or hybrid approach to his messages. Adams will also do book studies that he calls topical. These book studies may be broken down into smaller themes or topics like "Identity Theft," a study through the identity crisis many experienced when Jesus challenged their world and religious views in the Gospel of John.

In Monrovia, Maryland, Kevin Marsico also uses a blended approach. He will often go through a book, chapter by chapter, looking at the major themes and breaking the content down by various topics found in the biblical text. Marsico's method, which seems to be very effective in his church, is a good example of one of the many ways to slice up what it means to be an expository teacher. Like Marsico, Brad Edwards, the pastor to adults at Cherry Hills Community Church in Highlands Ranch, Colorado, generally does book studies, which he breaks down into smaller themes or topics.

Sometimes pastors using the approach described by Marsico and Edwards will term their style as expository. Many also call this approach a book-by-book or book-study method. Almost always the respondents to our survey actively using this method will break down their book study into smaller, more focused topics. These topics usually are referenced in the biblical text itself.

John Wiley, senior pastor of River Christian Fellowship in Raytown, Missouri, uses his topical messages to cheer people on. Wiley wants people to fall in love with Jesus, and he sees his messages as a major tool in this effort. When Wiley speaks at River Christian, he seeks to be transparent, without pretense or the air that he is better or more together than anyone else.

Of the young adult generation, Wiley feels pretty strongly that they don't want to be told "how to do something." Instead Wiley believes,

"They don't want to be told how to, as much as they want to hear about life experiences . . . victories, and struggles" faced by someone else.

Another topical pastor, Carlton Anderson of The River's Edge, Iowa Falls, Iowa, seeks to connect with his listeners by just "keeping it simple." Anderson often uses humor and simple language to engage people in a way they can understand.

Slightly less than half of the pastors we surveyed seemed to lean toward being more topical. Almost 50 percent of these topical pastors we surveyed also said they do studies of books of the Bible from a topical approach. At Cedar Creek Community Church in Perrysburg, Ohio, Lee Powell leads his church away from their typical topical model twice each year. During his twice-annual pilgrimage into a book or expositional series, Powell attempts to connect with his audience by pulling out major topics found in the text.

Occasionally Powell hears certain calls for his church to move almost entirely to an expositional model. Powell is pretty passionate in his response to those calling for such a change at Cedar Creek. His response to them is: "We are going to have this mix because we know that Jesus preached topically. Jesus never preached an expositional sermon in His life that I know of. He always preached topical and He used illustrations and stories."

Powell disclosed his own take on the argument that maturing or mature Christians need expository teaching, "I think that is a perceived need and not a real need." Again, this chapter isn't designed to argue for or against any one type of preaching. We are simply giving you input into what churches are doing when they are effective at reaching young adults.

Another church that has had great success in reaching young adults is the multisite Eagle Brook Church. At the Spring Lake Park Campus, Campus Pastor to Groups, Mark Lenz, seems most interested in his church's effectiveness at leading people to faith rather than waving the banner for one style or the other. In our survey Mark told us:

> So many of our messages are so good [at] being practical and
> easy to understand. I think that is a positive that draws a lot
> of young adults to Eagle Brook. Our messages are spoken in
> a language they can understand. It is music they can relate
> to. We will often . . . most every Sunday, have some sort of a
> video clip illustrating a point in the message, you know, from
> a TV show that they are familiar with.[5]

From our research most of the pastors using a blended or hybrid approach seem to be fans of simply connecting with people rather than waving the party colors of either the topical or expository camps. Each of these pastors would tell you he believes they're pulling out and using the best attributes of both message styles. One particular type of message that can sometimes fit in either the expository or topical categories is the narrative or storytelling style.

Putting an Exclamation Mark on Content Retention

Every school teacher and college professor knows the disappointment of lessons taught but never caught. Every mom and dad has watched as children ran full force into a painful trial that could have been avoided had the child listened to and heeded the guiding of their parents. In countless churches this weekend, millions of people will exit, never thinking twice about what was said by the pastor in his message. All the pastor's studying—the twelve, fifteen, or twenty hours of preparation—it can all be forgotten in five minutes.

From our surveys we noted a common goal of many churches is to get their people to connect with the message beyond the weekend service. One way churches are doing this is to have small groups unpack previous messages through group discussion, often with discussion guides posted on Web sites and blogs immediately following the weekend services. At C3 Church in Clayton, North Carolina, Matt Fry explained this message to small group connection this way, "We'll package a series together and our connect groups will typically be in sync with the sermons so their primary material will come from that Sunday's sermon or at least from the theme of that series."

Small groups are able to help people digest the weekend message, including assisting people with applying the message to their own lives. Our research has revealed that an increasingly large number of churches are doing this.

A Greater Purpose

Paramount to the way pastors deliver their content must be an answer to the question, "What is the purpose of the Scriptures?" Did Jesus come to this world to condemn the world? Or was Christ's purpose that by faith the world could be saved? Hint: You can find the answer in John 3:17.

Can a church be effective at reaching the lost and unchurched if it is more concerned with maintaining the approval of churched people than it is for teaching the Bible for faith? If delivering rousing messages for the approval of the Pharisees and other religious people was the primary purpose of Christ's coming to this world, what was the reason for Christ's incarnation in the first place?

I have never personally met anyone who would argue that Christ came to praise the Pharisees for how much they knew, or to affirm religious people in their religiosity. Yet the practice of countless churches reveals that we are doing the very thing that Jesus never did. Too many pastors are afraid of losing their jobs and never cross the line from preaching for church people to actually delivering messages for life transformation of both the lost and the saved.

Having beef in a hamburger doesn't mean it must always be Angus, though I love a good Angus burger. There really is no meat in a message if we are unfaithful to the Scriptures. Equally, there is no beef in a message if we give no thought to how to reach into the lost person's heart and stir them to faith as opposed to simply proving they are wrong.

Our job isn't to inhibit the work of God's Spirit as He draws people to Christ and convicts them of the truth. Instead, we are to join the Spirit in His activity. To do so means we must be biblically faithful in teaching the truth of God's Word while lovingly engaging the lost with that truth.

Communication That Connects Can Change Lives

Regardless of the way one feels led to deliver the content, constant recurring qualities found in leaders of churches reaching young adults include:

- belief that the Bible is true
- belief that Bible teaching can and should apply to real life
- belief that the message must speak to unbelievers
- belief that the pastor's message is either amplified or muted by everything else in a service
- belief in the need to grow as a Christ follower
- belief in the need to grow as a communicator
- belief that an effective communicator is authentic
- belief in being true to one's self as opposed to trying to speak like someone else

While not necessarily encouraging pastors to compromise the message of the Bible, many of the leaders we surveyed recalled the importance of studying the world in which people live. Some have termed this as "studying the culture." In a very real since, Jesus studied the culture.

Being God, Christ knew (knows) everything. As you follow Christ's teaching in the Gospels, you see where He used His knowledge of first-century Palestine to speak in stories they understood. He wasn't concerned with showing His academics and smarts, which were infinite no less. Jesus didn't feel pressure to use terminology to show He was learned. He spoke in the language people understood. Though He knew Greek (and every other language that had existed or would come to be), Jesus primarily spoke in the common language of His land, Aramaic. He wanted the people to hear the message, see provision of the Heavenly Father, and trust in faith.

We've all sat through messages and wondered who the speaker was trying to impress. If you're like me, you've heard messages where you would best understand the speaker if you had a dictionary or maybe even wireless access to Google.

Churches that are reaching young adults are led by leaders who know the value of speaking to people, not over people. These leaders not only believe the Bible, they highly value communicating the truth of God's Word in a way that connects with real life. These leaders love not only the people already in their churches, they love the lost and are discontent if they are not reaching them. Effective communicators are regularly reevaluating everything they do and say, seeking to heed Paul's warning to avoid being a stumbling block. They see the importance of avoiding stagnation, and they seek opportunities to grow in their faith and as communicators of that faith. As a result, people are turning to Christ and living increasingly changed lives.

12

How Churches Are Connecting Young Adults

A FEW MONTHS AGO I TRAINED ALL THE CHAPLAINS ASSIGNED to the Coast Guard. They were an intimidating bunch. Uniform and clearly disciplined. And they gave me a jolt when they jumped up as one when the admiral came in.

My orders were to teach them about "young adults." We talked about postmodernism, cultural shifts, and epistemology (how people gain knowledge). All fascinating stuff. But we kept coming back to technology—a lot. The personnel they serve is shaped by technology. Technology is not just a tool to them, it is part of their culture—a technoculture. And they are not alone.

If you've been around in church life long enough, you've heard all the warnings about technology, you know, "the tool of the devil." Many of us remember preachers ranting about the television being the devil's little soapbox. Is technology sometimes used for evil purposes? I don't mean a simple little practical joke where you sneak in a video phone to record your child's *American Idol* performance in front of the mirror. Like the old-timey preachers warned, can evil triumph through the use of technology? For the answer we have to look no further than the proliferation of sexually explicit material on the Internet. The answer, resoundingly, is yes.

Fearful of technology's dark side, churches have been notoriously late in engaging the culture through technology. While many pastors were still proclaiming the moral ills of watching "movie pictures," others were slowly waking up to the potential impact that technology would offer for the proclamation of the gospel.

With young adults increasingly choosing to forgo church involvement, many churches are waking up to the need to embrace technology as one more effective tool in reaching the unchurched. Jason Wilson, executive pastor of New Spring Community Church in Anderson, South Carolina, speaks of the importance for churches to engage culture with technology:

> People like myself are using technology in our everyday lives to grow and to learn, and it's equally as important for the church to utilize the tools God has given us in our culture today. And so we feel if the church isn't able to work as hard as the culture to utilize the tools God has given all of us, to reach more people for him, then we are going to lose out in the long run. We just don't want that to happen.[1]

You may remember the beginning of the 1998 movie *You've Got Mail,* when Kathleen Kelly (Meg Ryan) practically ignored her newspaper columnist boyfriend, Frank (Greg Kinnear), as he predicted that computers would bring about civilization's doom. Remember when Frank left the room? Kathleen went straight to her computer and began exchanging e-mails with a complete stranger—NY142, aka Joe Fox (Tom Hanks).

I'm sure you remember the first time you heard of e-mail. Go ahead, admit it, for those of you who are old like myself, you thought, *What do you mean I can instantly send mail without a postage stamp?* By the way, there was a day when college classrooms were filled with awe as professors in tech departments were heralding the news of a new technology called the World Wide Web. For others of you, you can't remember a time without e-mail and the Web.

But, either way, few churches realized the coming tide of rapid communication and its impact on reaching a growing movement of unchurched young adults. Now with the proliferation of homes sporting one or more computers, there are endless possibilities for churches to use technology to connect with unconnected people.

In *You've Got Mail*, Kathleen Kelly's employee, George (Steve Zahn) laments: "For me the Internet is just yet another way of being rejected by women." How can a bunch of circuit boards, electronic files, and Web codes possibly be used to connect people at such an emotional level?

Young adults have very little recollection of communication before e-mail. Now we would not know how to live without BlackBerries, iPhones, iPods, text messaging, Facebook, MySpace, and Twitter. *American Idol* has moved text messaging into the national spotlight, and presidential campaigns use social Web sites to spread the fever for change. So why wouldn't churches seek to embrace technology as a major means to the goal of saturating the planet with the gospel?

In our research I've discovered that a new generation of churches and a growing number of older churches are embracing technology for this very reason. More specifically, churches that are connecting with young adults are increasingly using all sorts of technology:

- church Web sites
- e-mail and IM
- video, video chat
- Web-based small groups
- blogs
- social networking sites (Facebook, MySpace, Twitter)
- e-invites and e-vites
- e-newsletters (and trashing paper newsletters)
- satellite
- podcasts
- vodcasts
- mp3
- Webinars

We've all spent endless workdays in front of a computer. We sometimes reduce the computer to an emotionless, connectionless zone of digits and keyboard dust. Surely the one-eyed monster found in millions of work cubicles couldn't be part of the solution for increasing connectivity and community in the church? After a long day of cubicle-itis, many of the people we are attempting to reach get in their cars for an isolated commute in a sea of cars, only to finally arrive home in time to shut out the world with the click of a garage button.

Web-Enhanced Community

But people need connection. Praise God it wasn't long after He made Adam that He also created Eve! In my studies I've confirmed what I believed to be true . . . many churches are increasingly attempting to offer Web-based environments to foster community, networking, and education. Are these techno churches substituting technology for community? Or are they simply building upon the same model of contextualized ministry seen in Christ, Paul, Wycliffe, Guttenberg, and Billy Graham?

Take for example Sojourn Community Church in Louisville, Kentucky. Just a few years ago founding pastor Daniel Montgomery, then twenty-five, described himself as the oldest in his congregation. Now eight years later and just two years into their first building, Sojourn continues to reach a younger crowd with an average adult age in the lower thirties. A major factor in Sojourn's brief history is how they connect young adults through their online community, CCB (Church Community Builder). Not a full-fledged social networking site, CCB is a simple tool used by Sojourn to foster community by connecting individuals to Sojourn's small groups, Group Life. The most basic of systems, posting information about Sojourn's Group Life, CCB simply provides a descriptor and invitation to Sojourn's small groups, complete with leader contact information and e-mail addresses. Sojourn uses technology as a tool to move the disconnected from Christ into relationships with those connected with our Lord.

New Song Community Church of Culver City, California, has a Web site that blends features of Facebook with YouTube. On this site members can blog, participate in online studies and discussion boards, or even post shout-outs to their friends. This practice of posting online studies is growing as churches seek new ways to create community for disconnected people and encourage believers in their spiritual growth.

Web Sites—A Great First Impression before the First Visit

Gone is the day when every Presbyterian church looks Presbyterian and every Methodist church looks Methodist. Today's churches are more diversified than ever. You can no longer expect the same songs, liturgies, or similarly designed messages from church to church within a given denomination. Aren't you glad? Additionally, with the rapidly growing rate of nondenominational churches and an increasingly de-churched, transitioning to a post-churched culture, potential visitors greatly value the ability to visit a church online. And they are doing it weeks, and sometimes months, before visiting in person.

Online messages, live-video feeds, and online ministry descriptors help potential visitors get a basic picture of a local church prior to a physical visit. Unchurched people who are one, two, or three generations removed from church have no idea what church is like, except based on what they heard from a friend, witnessed at a funeral, or saw on television. If for some reason they've come to believe that all Baptists are against everything (wonder where they ever got that idea?), then until they visit your church, they're going to assume that if Baptist is in your name, then you're like all those "critical, judgmental Baptists." The problem is, they're not going to visit your church because they are certain they already know who you are and what your church is about.

Online presence, however, can change everything. A quality, frequently updated Web site can help dispel myths and lead that person to visit your church and come face-to-face with the Savior.

Pete Wilson, senior pastor of Crosspoint Community Church in Nashville, leads his church to create and post videos online with the hope they become viral-type media. When creating a new series, Pete and his team intentionally create pieces not just for Sunday mornings but for Web-wide postings. Their clips are engaging, often funny, and high quality. In turn, members and attendees pass the videos on to their sphere of friends, both as e-invites and as posts on social networking sites like Facebook. Pete notes that Crosspoint's response rate from such invites far outweigh some of their past methods like mass mailers and church newsletters going out as snail mail.

Journaling

Some staff members are finding that online journaling gives those outside the faith a view into their personal world—allowing unchurched people to see the authenticity of believers living Monday through Saturday what they say they believe on Sunday. Dave Ferguson (daveferguson.org), lead pastor of Community Christian Church, Naperville, Illinois, and visionary for the NewThing Network, says of his own online journaling, "I think letting people know, here it is Monday, Tuesday, Wednesday, Thursday, Friday, and the stuff we're talking about on Saturday and Sunday shows I'm trying to live that faith out." Dave told me that online journaling gives you influence with outsiders. He speaks of leaders using the Web for "a ton [of] more ways to connect with the people in your church and even beyond your church, outside of what you get in a 30-minute" weekend message. When the leader journals, those inside the church draw closer to their pastors, and those outside the church gain confidence in the church as a place for people with real lives.

Internet-Based Campuses

In our research we confirmed that some churches have moved to creating Internet-based church "campuses." Dave Ferguson looks to the day when Community Christian Church has an online campus, "We are on the verge of taking that step and we're a little behind the curve there, but that's going to happen real soon for us." Ferguson and Community Christian Church are a part of a growing effort to connect with unchurched and disconnected young adults through what may become a wave of new Web-based campuses. We've come a long way since those early days when we first woke up to the message, "You've got mail."

Video in Worship

One of the ways churches are solving people's perceptions that the church is not authentic is through effective video usage. We all know that many outside the church believe they do not need to be lectured from the "fake preacher who's not got a clue of their world." More and more Christian leaders are finding video to be one more effective means of bridging the gospel message into the real world in which people live. Jesus Himself was a vivid storyteller, engaging people of His day in the common medium of His time—stories. Video is the younger generation's storyteller.

Of his church's use of videos in worship, both homemade and clips from popular culture, Ferguson says that "it lets people know you're grounded in real life." When we help someone transfer from being an anonymous person with anonymous struggles to being a person who sees his world, his joys, or his struggles, the questions and the fears that he is wrestling with appear before him on a screen in worship, he becomes more open to the message.

My own girls love to hear stories, be it snuggled up on the couch or at the end of their bed just before bedtime. They also love to watch television. Characters like Troy Bolton and the whole *High School Musical* cast, along with the cartoon characters Phineas and Ferb, have created a whole new culture in my home. Ever since the first silent movies rolled out, capturing American hearts with 5-cent picture shows in "Nickelodeans," our culture has connected with media that shows not only the Cinderella and Prince Charming life we all wish for, but also the life in which we all live with real trials, real joys, and real fears.

The Minneapolis Star Tribune[2] notes that Eagle Brook Church in Hugo, Minnesota, runs an average of eleven thousand each weekend, swelling to seventeen thousand on big weekends like Easter and Christmas. Like computer programmers or Hollywood set designers, the staff of Eagle Brook believes the smallest details make a world of difference in assisting them with their message. As noted in the *Star Tribune* article, Amy Anderson, executive director of worship, is quoted as saying, "We don't want anything, no matter how small, to knock the worshipers out of the mood of the service." Eagle Brook staffers take care of those small details in a big fashion during each Sunday's service in their state of the art control room, "Houston." Houston contains the gear that makes for a smooth service that is well rehearsed and intentionally planned, yet deliberately presented as spontaneous.

Mark Lenz, groups' pastor for the Spring Lake Park Campus of Eagle Brook Church, explains, "We realize we live in a tech age and young adults are especially used to that." Mark says of young adults, "They have a kind of MTV mentality of lots of camera angles and movement and things like that. So that's the style that they are kind of used to. And like I said, we just utilize or leverage technology to bring the gospel message in a clear and relevant way."

Lenz makes the point here and I will make it again later. Technology must always be a servant to the gospel. Don't fall prey to the temptation that you found a great clip that needs a sermon to go with it. We are reaching people for the gospel's sake and video is simply a useful tool in this technological age.

Text for Jesus

How would you like to get a text message from God? The Mill is a college and twentysomething gathering at New Life Church, Colorado Springs, Colorado. The leadership team at The Mill is constantly searching for ways to connect with their crowd—www.themillonline.org, Facebook, and texting are just a few. During one particular message series, "Just Text Me," The Mill's mix of twentysomethings were encouraged to text their answers to a poll of questions associated with the night's message. At the end of the last night of the series, all eight hundred-plus in attendance received a text reading, "I'm waiting to spend time with you, God."

Maggie Turner, events coordinator for The Mill thinks it is natural to use texting to communicate with her generation and those younger. Maggie told me, "I don't know anyone my age that has a landline. Everyone has cell phones, and so that's huge." Many young adults and teens not only text frequently, they actually prefer it over other forms of communication. The culture at The Mill proves that texting is one more way churches can engage a tech-savvy culture.

What Is the Main Thing?

In *You've Got Mail,* there came a point where Kathleen Kelly and Joe Fox moved from an anonymous and double-life, love-hate relationship, to a point where they were inseparably in love. During their turbulent anonymous e-mailing days, they stuck together by keeping to the basics of a surface level relationship. The lessons she learned are important for us today.

We must always keep our focus and energies on the main thing— honoring God by reaching the lost. An advocate of pretty much any technology that will help them fulfill the Great Commission, Scott Austin, pastor of Next Gen Ministries for Community Bible Church of San Antonio, Texas, refers to their use of technology as an "entry point." Scott says they "fire up pretty much anything that is out there," e-mail, Twitter, Facebook, MySpace, and even video that he says they project on "big old hogging [video] screens."

The proliferation of mega electronic retailers like Best Buy is proof that some are prone to take technology to the extreme. Scott cautions, "Technology doesn't make bad preaching good and it doesn't make a bad worship leader a good musician, and technology doesn't make people who don't want to connect, connect."

Scott remembers a time in ministry when he felt he had to have and use every kind of technology. Now Scott says, "I think we've slowed down a little bit from that," because he and his team have come to the philosophy that "technology is fine if it is effective for people." In other words, Scott is an advocate of keeping the mission ahead of the tools (or toys).

Dave Smith of The Chapel at Akron, Ohio, notes that they ha. gone through the gamut of different techno-media levels at The Chapel. Dave believes they had reached "a point where [the emphasis on technology] was probably becoming" more of a hindrance to their connection with the people God was bringing them. As a result Dave commented, "We almost went back to the other direction where we had very little [techno-media elements]. It was very low key, more of an ancient feel."

Having once experienced what he described as a "Postmodern Hangover" from a previous open source blog that went haywire with crazy postings due to a lack of sponsored oversight, Scott Austin has led his ministry to refocus on the main thing. He told me he wants their ministry "to be built around the same thing the church was built around two thousand years ago . . . going from home to home and doing their lives together and living in community and being connected." Now that's something worth texting to a friend (or if you're still not with it, just send the e-mail).

How Churches Are Being Cross Generational

WHEN WE DID OUR RESEARCH, WE FOUND MANY CHURCHES where older adults seemed to be the missing link. They were nowhere to be found—and it seemed like some of these churches did not want them there. It was like a Star Trek episode where everyone died before turning thirty years old.

We were also surprised at just how many churches have significant cross-generational representation. In the middle of the list of churches with cool names like Journey, Doxa, and the like, we found "First" church of such-and-such city on the list. In other words, the *majority* of churches reaching young adults were also ministering to older generations as well—they were multigenerational.

How can a church effectively blend together people of diverse age groups? Is it wise? Would churches that desire to reach young adults be more effective if they focused all of their energies on building a church of people age thirty-five and down? (Don't panic . . . since you are reading my book, I guess we can let you pass as a young adult at thirty-nine, or even fifty.) Maybe a better question would be: Is it biblically faithful for a church to focus on reaching one age group only?

Among the current hot trends in church growth, we hear a lot about churches that are creating small groups for people of similar stages in life. In many ways these small groups are more concentrated versions of the Sunday school model, where churches created classes based on age. Yet our research has revealed that fostering a diverse climate of cross-generational relationships has caused growth in a number of churches. After all, in the book of Acts we see great growth take place in the early church, and it was never limited to one particular age group. God sowed the seeds of the gospel among a diverse population, which would eventually span the globe.

Doing Cross-Gen Ministry without a Strategy for Cross-Generational Ministry

In our research we discovered that some churches are very intentional about creating an environment for cross-generational relationships, while other churches have been amazed to see this happen all on its own—a movement of God. When commenting on the cross-gen ministry at Crosspoint Community Church in Nashville, Tennessee, senior pastor Pete Wilson noted that they haven't been "real intentional about it." Crosspoint created several small groups that are age specific, but he noted that most of Crosspoint's small groups that they call "life groups" are multigenerational.

According to Pastor Pete Wilson, one of the great reasons for the success of Crosspoint's life groups is that people share life lessons and learn within cross-generational circles at the church. Even the eighteen-to thirty-five-year-old Crosspointers agree that this model has worked well for Crosspoint.

Who could have imagined? Didn't the Bible speak about this matter? Paul addresses cross-generational ministry in writing to his younger protégé Timothy, "Don't let anyone look down on you because you are young, but set an example for the believers in speech, in life, in love, in faith and in purity" (1 Tim. 4:12). In other places Paul called on the older women to walk alongside and train the younger women, while also calling for mentoring types of relationships to develop between younger and older men.

Many churches are relying on older, less intentional methods in order to blend varying age groups. Jake Stum, pastor to young adults at

First Baptist of Cleveland, Tennessee, cites events like holiday banquets as being a primary place where they bring the generations together. Community service events, though not necessarily planned that way, also tend to be multi-generational in scope at First Baptist.

Even without a well-developed plan for cross-generational ministry, we are glad to see that Crosspoint and First Baptist are seeing relationships built across the age groups. But do not give up on planning. Our survey findings reveal that the majority of churches that do not plan for cross-generational ministry do not experience cross-generational ministry. If you want to grow a garden but do not prepare the soil and plant the seed, all you have in the end is dirt and weeds. As reported by the majority of churches in our study, ministries that do not purposefully seek to link the younger and older generations are missing out on a great growth tool for attendance and a potent maturation tool for discipleship.

Can You Provide Multiple Worship Styles and Cross-Gen Ministry?

If you polled one hundred college students and one hundred senior adults as to their preference of music, you are certain to find college students trending toward contemporary music. The older crowd would likewise be more prone to listen to older melodies that, while perhaps cutting edge for their time (many remember when Elvis was thought to be ruining the country), are much more reminiscent of a day come and gone. My girls like everything Disney. Myself, born in the 1960s and raised in the seventies and eighties, I like eighties hair band ballads. And yes—I can still play many of them on my guitar.

Many churches recognize this principle. Some are intentionally carving out multiple worship services with distinct flavors of music. Perhaps, and maybe even in your church as well, this approach has led to a general separation of age groups for First Baptist Church of Cleveland, Tennessee.

Jake Stum told us that First Baptist is still discovering how to foster better cross-generational relationships, as his church's varying worship environments "has really split the generations." Thankfully, though, this hasn't been like a typical split in previous generations, where one crowd stomps off and creates Second "Unity" Baptist Church to the dismay of First Unity. Instead, at First Baptist Cleveland, the older generation mostly chooses the early service, the younger generation chooses the middle service, while a more middle-aged and mixed crowd chooses the late service. Thus, worship warfare has been minimized.

Back in the late eighties and nineties, many churches tried to blend old hymns with "new" choruses. Of course, many new churches were "planted" because of this. Now many have concluded that the only way to make everyone happy is to create separate services for traditional, blended, and a plethora of modern choices from country to rock, and even some with a little pop. Largely where these separate worship styles are created, church services will predominately take on the feel of one age group—senior, middle-aged, or young adult. How then can you mix up the age groups and foster relationships that are more biblical and cross generational in scope?

The Intentional Approach to Cross-Generational Ministry

Throughout the Scriptures, we see cross-generational ministry take place. God chose Moses at age eighty to lead Israel out of bondage, and Moses mentored the younger Joshua. From a very early age, Jesus was intentional about relating to people outside of His age group. In the temple we find the young Jesus reading from and teaching the Scriptures in the presence of His elders. There were no age requirements for the twelve apostles. The leaders of the church in Acts spanned the age spectrum. Seeing this as God's example of how He has worked among His people, then we should courageously engage in cross-generational ministry. But, as I've already pointed out, cross-generational relationships are more likely to happen when church leaders intentionally promote them.

Steve Derdowski, senior pastor of Ambassador Church in Littleton, Colorado, is one of many pastors leading the way in fostering an intentional environment where older and younger generations nurture one another. With a history of small groups that were segregated by age, Ambassador Church began to see the potential benefits of a more cross-generational approach. When discussing his congregation's reaction, Steve explained, "Both sides really saw the need of it, both the older generation and the younger."

Steve is unreserved in speaking about early difficulties when this approach was implemented. He says, "Initially, it took a little bit of pushing on our leadership team's part to encourage the [cross-generational] interaction, but once it started, it's been good."

I'm sure some of you still think this is crazy. How can I really expect younger people in their twenties, young moms with babies, or young singles still uninterested in settling down in marriage to connect in groups with church members who may seem disconnected by twenty or thirty years of life experience? Wouldn't that simply run young adults off from my church?

In its truest sense, it may seem counterintuitive to expect that people will rush to join something that seems a bit unnatural in our society. But a deeper look at the reality of culture reveals an underlying need. With corporate ladders to climb and portfolios to build, many young American parents are raising their little ones far from any semblance of family or grandparents. Like many in the ministry, my own girls do not know what its like to have family nearby.

The movie *The Perfect Storm* chronicled the 1991 event where three storm systems, including the remains of Hurricane Grace, merged off the coast of Massachusetts to form one enormous storm. In the midst of major North Atlantic shipping lanes, this unnamed storm's one hundred foot waves pounded on unsuspecting ships like the *Andrea Gail,* a small fishing vessel out for its last catch of the season.

Because cross-generational mixing is occurring less frequently than ever among American families, I believe these circumstances create a perfect storm of disaster for unsuspecting parents where families are missing out on generations of wisdom. Discerning church leaders should see this storm as a perfect opportunity for churches to come alongside young families. As younger people and families search for mentoring relationships and surrogate grandparents for their kids, your church can become a place of refuge, spiritual guidance, and emotional support. Our research has reaffirmed that many churches are stepping up to meet this critical need.

Chad Lewis, pastor of Group Life at Sojourn Community Church in Louisville, Kentucky, spoke to me about Sojourn Home, a ministry that intentionally fosters cross-generational relationships at Sojourn Community Church. Chad says, "With Sojourn Home, we are actually pulling (older members) on board to be parent mentors." Older mentors meet with and mentor parents of young children. Additionally, Sojourn Home provides training for mentors wishing to become marriage counselors. These marriage mentors have been very effective in counseling younger married couples that are struggling, as well as carrying the load for providing Sojourn Community Church's premarital counseling.

If you are an older person visiting Sojourn, look out! Chad says, "When people come in and they are a little bit older, we kind of move in on them pretty quickly, just trying to engage them in conversation, just asking them about life, [and their] ministry experience." They place a high value on finding and equipping older members who will buy into the church's vision to lead younger generations as group leaders, mentors, and counselors.

The apostle Paul writes of the church in terms of a body. We're interconnected. Imagine those young singles looking for wisdom, a young couple in need of counseling, a single mom in need of a baby-sitter and someone to hold adult conversations with. These are real people who have real needs, and God has sent them your way. In this relational "perfect storm," an astounding opportunity is presented to your church—find and equip the older generation, many of whom need someone who needs them, for the purpose of investing in and meeting the needs of a new generation.

Many congregations are aiming to function like things will be in heaven because the church is to be a sign of the kingdom of God on earth. Resisting the urge to market their church toward one group to the exclusion of others, churches like Community Bible Church in Stockbridge, Georgia, seek to reach multiple generations with the gospel. Community Bible has recognized the value of multiple services with varying styles aimed at reaching a particular group of people, yet this church is also intentional about linking the generations.

For Community Bible Church, small groups are mostly defined by location or interests, rather than age. Senior Pastor Beau Adams remarks, "We mix people up in a big way and get them serving alongside of one another." In doing so, Beau says that the people "realize [Community Bible Church] is not a church of just age, but the body of Christ is much bigger and broader and there [are people] with varying perspectives."

Additionally, many of the church's events are specifically geared to bridging the generations. Part of Community Bible Church's cross-gen strategy involves local community service opportunities and special events where kids are linked up with grandparent figures for fun outings like fishing. Beau is onto something.

While we are not against grouping people together who are in similar stages of life, we do believe that the biblical evidence suggests that no person should live as an island unto themselves. God's intention is for the body of Christ, young and old, to be intricately linked in relationships of dual need and benefit. Adams put it this way:

Well, something has bothered me for a long time and it seems to be that in church we . . . for quite a while, we have had people coming in and immediately the first thing we do is we categorize people and we cubbyhole them. We put them where we think they should go. What we are finding out is that is not what they are looking for, but they are looking for something richer and fuller, and one of the things that excites me is a lot of these young teenagers that grew up in homes that were broken, that were falling apart, they have this desire for community and we have grandparent figures who have grandkids and who do not live nearby, but they love to be able to connect and meet with them; and these generations have so much to give to each other and they find that it is so much better together rather than being separated out and with people your own age only all the time.[1]

For Beau, the home unit, the family, is vital. Even so, Beau believes the Christian family as God intended it, must be so much more. He says of the family, "It is about people connecting regardless of whether they are really related or not, but becoming that family or the real family of God, the family of the church."

Becoming Intentional about Cross-Generational Ministry

Some of the churches that are best at reaching, keeping, and maturing young people intentionally build a system for linking the younger generations with the older ones. Others are churches that didn't necessarily begin with a high value for cross-generational ministry, yet they came to adopt it through some unforeseen trigger or crisis.

For instance, during a time of unprecedented rapid growth in college-aged students at The Church in West Ridge, Illinois, Senior Pastor Chad Runge discovered a conflict within his church. The church's worship pastor, himself a college student, began inviting his friends to church. Within two weeks the college population at The Church grew from five to sixty.

Chad told our team, "The old people freaked out because they weren't used to seeing all these young people. We got a lot of flack." Chad was proactive in encouraging older members to engage the new college students flooding their church. As a result, an initiative was created to match people over age fifty with college students in a grandparent/grandkid kind of relationship. This called for older members to adopt college students. How did they do this at The Church? To put it bluntly, Chad simply said, "We made them."

Based upon intentionally fostering these new cross-generational relationships at The Church in West Ridge, other new ministry initiatives are being born. One recently widowed eighty-year-old adoptive grandmother, Ruth, took six college girls under her wings. Ruth and her late husband never had children, so they traveled the world. Ruth is an avid storyteller, and her adopted college-aged girls love listening to her stories about traveling the world. Chad spoke of the desire among Ruth's "girls" to assist with digging wells in Africa and providing malaria nets in Morocco. Ruth simply told them, "Get your passport and go."

Moreover, Ruth is leading her family of adopted, college-aged granddaughters to do ministry on a local basis to shut-ins and other older people, some younger than Ruth. Having come from a younger church in Florida, Chad discovered a need to minister to older people through a regular visitation ministry at The Church.

Unlike the typical, modern, American model that treats some people as less important because of their increased age, Chad made the right call. Besides leading the church's older members to embrace college students, he also had the guts to require the older church members to minister to their own generation. Speaking to this, Chad said, "The challenge was that they expected the pastors to do all the work, and so, we looked at all the older people that had relationships with these shut-ins and said it is not our job. It's your job. They are your friends. You need to love them and take care of them. Now, we are going to help you do that."

Now, assisted by a staff intern, Ruth and her adopted girls are leading their church in connecting with older people through home, hospital, and nursing home visits. In summary, Chad recalled, "We challenged the students to cherish and honor the older generation," and they got it.

Cross-Generational Small Groups

How do you do cross-generational small groups? Well, first let us encourage you to read Randy Frazee's book *The Connecting Church*, which is frequently mentioned when discussing cross-generational small groups. After receiving some insights from those who have done it well, begin to shape a portrait of the future where generational lines are blurred for ministry purposes. As your church begins to discover how ministry can happen among *all* age groups, begin to look for a vehicle that can facilitate the ministry. Small groups can be the ministry where relationships naturally develop and life is shared across the generations. Here are some thoughts on what delineates cross-generational small groups:

- Transcend age
- Benefit from life experience of older adults
- Benefit from energy and passion of younger adults
- Provide a natural conduit for mentoring the next generation of leaders
- Provide child-rearing assistance for younger adults
- Provide appreciation and the sense of being needed for older adults
- May be linked by geographical location
- May be linked by interests or hobbies
- May be linked by a desire to study a particular book of the Bible
- Strengthen the overall ministry of the church
- Provide needed group care and pastoral type shepherding

For most people who have attended church for a while, small groups that cross generational lines will be completely different from age-graded Sunday school groups. Therefore, continue to paint the picture of how your church can minister to the lost in your community. People are seeking to establish new family connections that jobs, moves, transfers, and going to college have wrenched from their lives. These relationships can become the bridge that God uses to communicate the gospel.

Why My Church Should Become More Cross Generational in Practice

If you have read much of my work, you know that I am not opposed to using proven tools of marketing as part of a comprehensive outreach and evangelism strategy. I believe that churches should be concerned enough about the unchurched to do everything they can to introduce the lost to faith in Christ. If churches are unwilling to do that, they are missing the gospel.

However, it is also apparent to me that sometimes we go too far and become blinded by the practices of modern corporate marketing, fooling ourselves into thinking that we can be kingdom churches without doing the kingdom thing . . . reaching out to all. If we are reaching out to all, we must consider how we can grow our people, young and old, to look more like a biblical body of interlinked pieces, woven together by the Chief Architect into the body of Christ.

Take a look at that body for just a moment—the hands, the feet, the limbs, the mouth. Those parts all join together by design, for purpose and function. The parts of our body also work together because they need each another.

Some older people feel that they have nothing left to give; they feel they are no longer valued or wanted. Many have grown kids who are too busy to call or too calloused to care. They watch alone as their closest friends and family members pass from this life.

But, these precious, older "family members" have needs—they long to be engaged and valued. With a wealth of life experience, their depth of wisdom is greater than any self-help book. They wish they could make a difference and feel the pride of walking with another person through a critical time or decision. Many long for the warmth of an embrace and the assurance of a smile returned.

Some younger people in your church feel overwhelmed at the decisions before them. Sometimes they are too cocky and self-assured for their own good or their family's good. But, they're probably not too far from a huge crisis . . . getting fired, a contract falling through, a child's rebelliousness, the pain of bankruptcy, or the strain of infidelity.

Countless young adults wish they had someone who could help them understand their parents or maybe someone who can help babysit the kids, not for money but for love. It is likely that a young person will attend your church this Sunday, and they wish that they had someone whom they could trust to guide them in relating to a prodigal child or hold their hand through a sickness.

I've described two groups of people who need one another, and yet the normal response by church leaders is to isolate these groups into separate realms of church life. As such, these churches and their people miss developing memorable relationships, and the impact of the church is lessened. Somehow I can't help but think that the light of the church is somehow dimmed.

It will take boldness to begin linking these two groups, but the overwhelming findings of our study reveal that cross-generational ministry can be one of the greatest and most accessible assets you have for strengthening the growth of your church. With a growing army of baby boomers moving into retirement, now is the time for cross-generational ministry.

How Churches Are Being Authentic

HOW DID WE GO FROM *FATHER KNOWS BEST* TO *HOGAN KNOWS Best* in such a short time? I remember the anticipation I felt as the school day was ending, anticipation building in me. BUZZ—drop the books in the locker, try to sneak past the older jocks, and run back home from Wisdom Lane Elementary in Levittown, New York. In third grade I always worried I would not make it home in time. Why the urgency? *The Andy Griffith Show* was on. I had to make it home in time for the opening scene. You know the scene—it's the one that sets up the whole episode, usually when Opie did something bad or Barney did something silly.

What is it about today's reality television that draws people in by the droves? What is it about a TV show that would cause someone to tune out the melody of their own life, only to be replaced by the noise and chaos of over-produced drama? Perhaps the answer is what entertainment executives are banking millions of corporate sponsored dollars on. Hint: It's the same thing that drew me to that little town of Mayberry twenty-five years ago—CONFLICT.

In his book *5 Dysfunctions of Team*, Patrick M. Lencioni writes about how conflict is the thing that really draws in an audience and that leaders should mine for it in their meetings. He goes on to assert that an organization that embraces healthy conflict can achieve a sustained competitive advantage, increase productivity, increase morale, and even reduce turnover.[1]

So what is it about conflict that is so compelling? It is raw. It is unpolished. It makes things real. It is the foundation of what I believe we all seek after—authenticity.

Authentic

Dictionary.com Unabridged (v 1.1)
au·then·tic • [aw-then-tik] –adjective

- not false or copied; genuine; real: *an authentic antique.*
- having the origin supported by unquestionable evidence; authenticated; verified: *an authentic document of the Middle Ages; an authentic work of the old master.*
- entitled to acceptance or belief because of agreement with known facts or experience; reliable; trustworthy: *an authentic report on poverty in Africa.*[2]

Authenticity is proven, and it is challenged. In relationships it is wrestled for—whether with self or with others. It is the wrestling that keeps us tuned in week after week, keeps us on the edge of our seats, and moves our hearts.

Lost and Found is about churches that are reaching young people and how they do that. And authenticity came up. Not once. Not a lot. But always.

One hundred percent of churches interviewed, deemed effective at reaching young people by our criteria, hold authenticity as one of their highest values or has a commitment to being authentic.

Matt Chandler, a friend and pastor of The Village Church in the Dallas area, responded to my question about why it was so important. He explained, "The gospel ushered in authenticity. That openness about where we all were, what we were struggling with, and our deep need for Jesus made the church a safe place for people to come."

The last time I was at Matt's church it had two thousand in attendance. Today, just a few years later, it has six thousand—mostly young adults. However, Matt explains that it is not just a young adult thing:

Del Steele was a seventy-year-old deacon who shared his testimony about a year in to our journey. One Sunday morning he got up and shared that he had grown up in church, was a head deacon, but never had a relationship with Christ. He had spent his life just trying to be good and do what was right. He then talked about the saving power of grace and the joy of walking with Christ. This blew up the religious paradigm that had historically been present and pushed us into being a gospel-centered place. Dozens accepted Christ in the weeks following his testimony.[3]

Young people are desperately seeking something real, something authentic—and they don't mind if it is messy. They expect it to be messy. Furthermore, if it is not messy, they question its authenticity. Without the conflict they are less likely to be drawn in. Thus the rise of reality television, and also the effectiveness of churches that engage in messy ministries to the inner-city poor, homeless, addicted, and others.

A number of the leaders we talked to share a common voice regarding young people observing so much scandal and hypocrisy. They all agreed that this has led to today's young adults' fear and distrust of anything that appears polished or rehearsed. We can again see clues of this in pop culture with the popularity of movies such as *The Blair Witch Project* or *Clerks*. User-driven media and social networking Internet sites show that the younger generation is willing to lose on the "production" end to gain authenticity.

Chad Runge, senior pastor of The Church in West Ridge (Chicago), Illinois, had this to say when asked why he thought authenticity was so important to the young adults in his church . . .

Because they can't . . . I mean, and don't take this the wrong way, but they can't connect with Joel Osteen. Connecting with him is like connecting with Alex Rodriguez or Jerry Springer or Matt Damon. He's just another face on a TV screen.[4]

He was not alone in his sentiment that young adults have a hard time relating to the "superstar" pastor. Many of those interviewed said that the pastor must be someone they can relate to and that what helps them relate most is authenticity.

Chad went on to say that young adults want to relate, and what helps them relate is the drama of conflict, which is the purifying agent of authenticity . . .

And so they want it [authenticity] . . . they want to see that
people struggle, that people fight sin, and that people go
through stuff; that there is redemption and restoration; and
that Jesus is real and not some superstar.[5]

Pete Wilson, senior pastor of Crosspoint Community Church in
Nashville, Tennessee, expressed that at his church they constantly reaf-
firm people's authenticity explaining, "It can't be an add-on or an extra.
They may put up with a lot they don't like, but they will not tolerate
an inauthentic leader."

So what makes an authentic leader? According to our interviews
authentic leaders are people who:

- lead from brokenness
- are not afraid to share their struggles
- are willing to tell stories that may make them appear weak or
  imperfect
- avoid pretenses or the use of gimmicks
- admit the need for grace and for a Savior
- are hopeful about the redemption they have found in Jesus

These markers are important because it is contrary to what I was
taught in seminary—and I am guessing it is different than what you
might have learned as well. For many who adopted the corporate model
of leadership prevalent in the last few decades, showing weakness invites
unwanted criticism and castigating judgment of others. By default,
most leaders attempted to show a "perfect life" portrait of their family,
devotional prowess, and personal holiness. Today's younger generation
will be repulsed and see it as self-delusional arrogance.

Of course, when you're an authentic leader, you are generally not
showing secrets—many (if not most) people already know your faults.

When I turned forty, I sent out forms to fifteen of my friends
who worked for me and people for whom I worked asking them to
do an "evaluation" of me. I wanted to know what I needed to work
on.

Overwhelmingly the comments came back that I was too sarcastic
and did not listen well. (I told them they were big jerks, and I did not
believe them.)

OK. Not really. But, I said to my wife, "Honey, I think the Lord
is pressing on me to be less sarcastic and to try to listen better. I think
I have a problem in that area."

Her response was priceless. She looked at me and said (with a smile), "And this is news to you?"

It was. Well, not completely new news. But I was surprised at it. And when I shared my struggle at church, they all nodded and said, "We're glad Ed is finally seeing it." When I am authentic, and confess my struggles, it is liberating to the people who know me. Steve Holdaway, senior pastor of West Bellevue Church (of Lifespring Church) in Bellevue, Nevada, explains it rather simply, "They want to know that he hurts like they hurt and mess up."

Or, another way to put it might be from Adam Edgerly, pastor of NewSong Community Church in Culver City, California. He explained that their motto says they are "a church of misfits." As leaders at his church, he feels like they're a "group of broken people." They try to lead from a place of weakness being mended; it helps people be open and comfortable with them.

There is a powerful scene in *Black Hawk Down* that might help. Lt. Col. Danny McKnight is in a fierce battle. The transport is filled with the wounded and there is blood everywhere. He yells at Private Othic, "You, get up there and drive!" Othic pleads, "But I'm shot, Colonel!" McKnight could speak for us all when he says, "Everybody's shot!"

Everyone is shot—and it's OK to be honest about it. One pastor explained, "If people can't see your passion or struggle about an issue, then why should they believe you?" Yet he also cautioned, "Story is important, but in order to be authentic, it must be your own story." Would a leader really tell a lie in order to appear authentic? This is a huge trap for leaders who want to find creative ways to connect with their audience.

Ironically there is little *real* about "reality television." Authenticity cannot be manufactured. Authenticity must be discovered, cultivated, and shared.

Imagine authenticity as a three-legged stool that the church must be able to put all of its weight on. If one of the legs is broken, the load topples. Discovery, cultivation, and sharing are those legs.

Discovery

As I stated earlier, 100 percent of churches interviewed, deemed effective at reaching young people by our criteria, hold authenticity as one of their highest values.

Let's think about values for a minute. I propose a simple definition: A value is a hill you or your organization are willing to fight for and/or die on. Values are not the same as goals. Values are what drive you to reach your goals. They are the guardrails that keep you on the road.

One thing I have learned in ministry is that in every church there are *actual* values and there are *aspirational* values. Actual values are discovered about one's organization and aspiration values are dreamed of but rarely actualized.

If you have ever spent any time talking to anyone on staff at Willow Creek Community Church in South Barrington, Illinois, about leadership, you have probably heard them mention the book *Built to Last: Successful Habits of Visionary Companies* by James Collins and Jerry Porras. This book makes the argument for the need to have a clear mission and vision that is guided by *discovered* actual values. It encourages you to ask questions like, "Do my thoughts, words, and actions indicate that _____ is really something I value?"

Self-examination seasoned with brutal honesty is a must for discovering one's values. Once you think you know what you value, then you are ready to ask the really tough question, "Would those who really know me agree that this is something I value?" So back to the idea of authenticity, would the people in your organization agree that *authenticity* is one of your values? Ask them.

Cultivation

When I think of the word *cultivation*, I think of farming. Not the modern diesel-fueled, fully-automated kind. No, the kind that brings memories of Amish families turning their soil equipped with burlap sacks for weeding and horse-drawn plows for tilling. The kind of farmers that showed love, care, and respect for the land, because it was that very land that was taking care of not only their family, but also those around it.

For some the cultivation of authenticity can be a mechanical process. Especially for those leaders who are uncomfortable with the idea. In my experience the mechanically produced crops may produce a higher yield, but in the area of authenticity they tend to be weak and lack the genuine flavor of their hand-tended counterparts. Metaphorically speaking, effective churches have realized that genetically altered, chemically treated, and mass produced corn is OK for the big-box super stores but not for them. They would much rather visit a farmer's market, pay a little more, and know that when they get their fresh-picked corn home, it will be deliciously sweet, unquestionably pure, and will have supported local farmers who have their well being in mind.

The cultivation of soil and of authenticity requires the three same basic requirements:

Basic requirement:	Soil	Authenticity
The right environment	water and sunshine	humility and honesty
The right nutrients	fertilizer	encouragement
The right tools	farmer and tiller	God and community

Humility and honesty play a key role in setting an environment for authenticity. When people are free to be who they are and know they'll be loved despite their flaws, they are in an environment that invites growth and are more likely to flourish. Conversely, implementing the right tools—God and community—will guard us from a false humility (which is pride in disguise) that simply wishes to gush out our pain so people will be drawn to our vision.

According to Greg Byman, senior pastor at St. Joe Community Church in Fort Wayne, Indiana, there is an environment of authenticity that has produced a sense of freedom in the lives of their people to be who they really are. "Real people, Real church, and Real God" is their motto. For them it expresses a willingness on the part of the church to meet people right where they are. Their goal is to develop people, and they do it personally. For example, their life development class is taught personally by the pastor. They do this to avoid a sense that the pastor is untouchable.

We obviously try to remain very transparent in who we are and the way we engage people. Authenticity comes in many forms. It comes in the forms of willingness to engage people where they are, to accept people where they are, to challenge people in ways they need to be challenged, to remove as many man-made barriers as possible, and to engage them in relationship. Our goal is not to get a bunch of numbers in there, but to develop a bunch of people and to know them personally.[6]

Authenticity is something you have to dig for, to be willing to work hard for, and you have to be willing to get some dirt under your nails. Ask anyone who experiences it in their community, and they will tell you how delicious the real thing is.

Sharing

It only takes a spark to get a fire going. Don't worry, I'm not quoting the bad campfire song. And I'm not referring to wildfires in California. What I am referring to is the idea that once authenticity has been discovered and is being cultivated, it is a fire that rages deep in the hearts of those in its path.

What I mean is . . . Once you've tasted an organic Honeycrisp Apple grown by a guy you met in the Muddy Pond Amish Community just outside Monterey, Tennessee, it's hard to swallow a wax-polished, pesticide-tainted knockoff from the supermarket. Can you tell I'm on a farming kick?

Seriously though, once someone has the guts to be real and put themselves out there, it inspires others to want to do the same. But in church that could open up a huge can of something! My research shows that young people want to be known—really known. They want to be loved despite the jerk they can be sometimes.

In a painful world, sharing struggles without bumper-sticker answers is essential. The new generation wants to honestly share and be thoroughly heard. They desperately want to share burdens with one another.

What if the church was a safe place for hurting people to come, be themselves, share their junk, and be loved anyway? Young people all over the country are looking to connect with that kind of church family. It is where they envision growing to be more like Christ.

So, what is it that keeps that from happening? What is keeping churches from experiencing the kind of authenticity that could break through social, racial, demographic, and psychographic barriers? Some would say it is the desire for the church or more realistically the pastor to be seen as the model of stability. Pastors are supposed to have it all together and their families are supposed to have that Rockwellian glow about them. Right? Have you seen my kids? Better yet, have you seen me, with my kids on Sunday morning, just before giving a message on patience?

Others would say it is fear. Fear that somehow the pastor has a weak faith or that the church is weak on tough issues. Still others might say it is arrogance, pride, or self-righteousness.

I know it is not like me to do this, but I am going to be a little controversial. I am going to go out on a limb and say that one of the biggest causes of a lack of authenticity in churches today is when a church values excellence over honesty. OK—there—I said it. Excellence can be an authenticity killer.

"Finally, someone from the big church world has the guts to say it." Some of you are remembering your last vision retreat when you wrestled with this internally but were afraid to say anything for fear that being real with other staff members might reveal a weakness that would later be exploited. And if you are one of the people who was so distracted by the awesome light show at your last service that you missed the woman sitting in the third row crying during that last verse of "Amazing Grace," you might want to back up a few paragraphs and try again.

Now wait a second. Before you go looking for the matches and kerosene, hear me out. I am NOT saying we shouldn't do things with excellence. We should. We should give God our best in everything we do. Absolutely. But that commitment to personal excellence should include the transparency we have with one another. Where we mess up is when what we say (or more often do) communicates that someone's best is not good enough.

When our desire to appear excellent or polished outweighs our desire to be seen as broken, fallen sinners in desperate need of God's redemptive gift of grace, there is a real problem.

Who would you relate to better: the guy who appears to have it all together or the guy who occasionally questions what the heck God is up to?

As you can tell I am spending a lot of time talking about the idea of sharing as it relates to authenticity. The reason for this is that of the three supporting legs I mentioned above, sharing takes the prize for being most likely to succeed (at failing the church).

James 5:13–20 is an oft-wrestled-over passage regarding prayer and healing. It would be wise of us to take note that it is within James's admonition for us to pray with faith that he also says, "Therefore confess your sins to each other and pray for each other so that you may be healed. The prayer of a righteous man is powerful and effective" (v. 16). In the most personal issue of life, confessing our faults should be the natural habit of the believer.

What will it take? One leader willing to be vulnerable can bring a sense of freedom to a congregation caged by fear. Imagine years of frustration with God over an unhealed family member being spoken aloud so the rest of the body can encourage, pray for their pain to subside and their own heart be healed. Imagine addictions being brought out into the light, fears being fought, relationships being restored—all because it is OK to admit that sometimes there is junk in our lives, sometimes the Christian life is not a bed of roses. Have you ever seen a rosebush? Did you notice all those pointy things on the stems?

Here is the hard part—it has to start with the leaders.

Henri Nouwen spoke these words many years before his death in 1978, but they hold even truer for our church leaders today:

"What Is Most Personal, Is Most Universal"[7]

Today's Christian leader is faced with the task of trying to make the greatest impact possible on the greatest amount of people possible, in the shortest amount of time possible. To effectively reach young adults, leaders must be willing to examine their own lives for an Authenticity Deficit Disorder. Be advised, this form of ADD is not genetic, is socially contracted, and is highly contagious. It especially has no mercy on bald guys with soul patches.

By now you may be asking yourself, and I hope you are, "Am I an authentic leader?"

Here are a few questions to ask yourself (I shouldn't have to say this, but be honest):

- Do my words and actions communicate to others my desire to be real?
- Do I do or say things to cause reactions or elicit responses from others?
- Do others see me as someone they can relate to?
- Do my words and actions say the same thing?
- Do others see me as someone with depth?
- Am I the same in front of people as I am alone?
- Do I ever say or do things for shock value?
- Would my friends agree with my answers above?

How did you do? If you are like most, you will recognize a few areas of your life that could use some work. Your first assignment is to go and *share* that with someone you trust who will encourage you toward authenticity.

OK, we have picked on leaders enough. Let's get back to talking more specifically about how churches *are* being authentic. Peter Ahn, senior pastor at Metro Community Church in Fort Lee, New Jersey, talks about personal things during his messages and how that impacts the listener's walk with Christ, which in turn impacts their church:

We try to make the sermons very applicable through authenticity and transparency. I use a deep level of sharing in order to identify with others (coming from a broken home with an abusive father and things like that). I think if people can connect with me and see that I've had to deal with similar struggles, it demonstrates the hope that Jesus provides in the midst of pain as opposed to just the pastor talking about hope.

So we believe in sharing personal stories and tying them into the messages. Pain resonates with people; it doesn't discriminate.

So if we can come together with a commonality being not our strengths, but our weaknesses, I think our generation longs for community like that. The church is not a place where we come together because we have these great gifts. But rather we come together because we are broken people and we are misfits.

So that's the ministry philosophy of our church. And I find that a lot of young people are hurting. Many of them are still hurting from the absence of parents who worked all day when they were kids. They grew up feeling alone and abandoned.

I think God does something special in a community when we come together through our pain.

It takes time, though. I think you can grow a church much quicker if you talk about a prosperity gospel and things like that. But one of the main values of our church is being authentic and with that being open about the things we go through in life and our own brokenness. That helps us to be more compassionate in our understanding toward other people, especially the ones who come into our church.[8]

I remember the first time I ever saw Aunt Bee cry. I'll never forget it, because on that day I saw her as a real person. A big parade was to be planned and everyone was counting on her to put it all together. The decorating, organizing, cooking, and hosting all fell on her. As usual she was afraid to say no, afraid to ask for help, afraid to look weak.

A typical Barney mishap brought it all crashing around her. As she broke down she finally admitted it was not "all good," it was not "fine." She cried, and I cried with her. It was then that everyone finally rallied around her, pitched in, and the parade was a huge success (a lot better than if she had done it herself).

Authenticity changes everything.

How Churches Are Leading with Transparency

WHO IS A LEADER THAT ALLOWS THE LIGHT TO SHINE THROUGH his or her life?

In the movie *The Matrix*, Neo becomes the leader of a group that rebels against the machines. By creating a simulated reality, these machines are pacifying and subduing the human population in order to use the humans for body heat and electrical activity. As Neo learns to resist the machine matrix, he becomes "the One." This happens when the matrix becomes transparent to him; Neo sees it for what it really is—lines of streaming green code. This gives him the ability to manipulate the matrix and defeat its agents.

At the end of the movie, Neo hacks into the matrix. He makes a telephone call promising he will demonstrate to the people imprisoned in the matrix that anything is possible. He has seen the light, so to speak, and he wants others to see the light as well.

The younger generation wants to see the light, and they want to follow authentic leaders who will show them the way. Younger adults are not interested in following leaders who are unwilling to take a real look at themselves or who are unwilling to open their eyes to real needs in the real world.

A transparent leader sees things as they really are, personally and in the world. Then leaders who are transparent let the light of that reality shine through their lives in a way that frees others. Transparent leadership is not about "letting it all hang out" without any consideration of how being open and honest will impact others. Leading with transparency involves self-awareness, vulnerability, and taking responsibility for one's self and toward others.

In an earlier chapter, we discussed the reality that younger adults place great value on authenticity. While authenticity and transparency are similar traits, they are not the same.

In this chapter we describe the importance of leaders being transparent in churches. In many of the interviews we did with church leaders, we heard how important this issue is in reaching young adults.

When asked about the importance of leading with transparency, the pastor of Riverpoint Church in Newton, Kansas, explained it this way:

> When I'm up preaching and any time I'm trying to put some life application in it, and if they know me and know what I am going through, they can relate better. If you're open with them and honest with them, they are going to be more apt to trust you as a leader, as a speaker.
>
> I think that helps me in my communicating God's Word, because I am trying to be real and to let them know that, hey, I mess up on these things, too, you know. I fail at this stuff, too. So, we're in this together. Let's go forward together. It's just . . . I don't think they see me as someone who is on a pedestal. They just see me as their pastor, as their leader. But do you know what? We are all trying.[1]

Transparent leadership helps build genuine connections with followers and allows people to feel like they are not alone in their life struggles. It is easier to trust leaders who don't try to pretend that they have it all together. But this doesn't mean that leaders have to go around telling everybody all of their problems.

What Does It Mean to Lead with Transparency?

Let's start off with a simple definition of *Leadership Transparency* and then discuss how you get there. We've all heard it many times, but it's still true—leadership is influence. Leadership is about motivating people to achieve meaningful and purposeful things in their own lives and also in the lives of others. Being transparent literally means to "allow the light to shine through." Put them together—leadership transparency is influencing others to change and make an impact by allowing the light to pass through who you are.

Certainly one person who achieved that was Jesus. When He lived on the earth, Jesus became the leader of a movement. That movement started with twelve followers and eventually spread around the world. It spread through ordinary people. How did He do it? How did He exert such great influence on His followers and motivate them to make personal changes and impact the world?

Not only was Jesus a leader—He was a transparent leader. He was honest. He expressed emotions like compassion, anger, joy, and frustration. He laughed, and He cried. He was real, authentic, and genuine. He told it like it was, even when the disciples and others didn't want to hear it.

From the human side, Jesus "let it all hang out" at times. He displayed righteous anger when people were misusing the temple courts in Matthew 21. He displayed deep compassion and love when He wept over the people of the city of Jerusalem (see Luke 19) and over His good friend Lazarus's death (see John 11). Luke 10 tells us that Jesus was full of joy.

From the divine side, Jesus was willing to display who He really was as well. The most dynamic occasion involved the three closest of His twelve disciples—Peter, James, and John (see Matt. 17). This was an occasion when Jesus let His divinity shine through. All of those occasions, both human and divine, help describe what it means to be transparent—allowing the light to shine through who you are. Jesus clearly displayed who He was and what was important, and He always did so with purpose. It was not for show or manipulation or attention.

Jesus made an impact while He was on earth, and others followed Him to do the same. He led a movement to change lives and change the world. And this One, the only One who is fully God and fully man, did it by leading with transparency.

In part, transparency has to do with being open and honest, but it is more than that. It involves being open and honest with a purpose—a purpose that is redemptive and developmental, a purpose that allows the light to shine through who you really are so that others are impacted in positive ways.

Being transparent is allowing others to look into and through your life, displaying a window to your soul. But the leader who is being transparent opens that window for the divine and pure purpose of helping others change in positive ways, without hidden motives or pretense. Those windows are also opened to move people to meaningful action. That is the kind of transparency that will connect with younger adults.

When the light of God's presence is allowed to shine through your life, people not only see your faults and failures, but they will also see the presence of Jesus changing you to become more like Him. That gives people a real sense of hope that God can change them too, and it can motivate people to share that presence with other hurting people and for the purpose of meeting real needs.

Now let's talk about some ingredients for leading with transparency. What does it take to be a leader who lets the light shine through his life? What will happen when you begin to mix those ingredients together?

Ingredients for Leadership Transparency

Leading with transparency will require that leaders practice self-awareness, vulnerability, careful honesty, time, and real excellence.

Self-Awareness

The first ingredient is practicing self-awareness. In his book *Practicing Greatness*, Reggie McNeal lists this as the first discipline of extraordinary leaders. He states, "Without appropriate self-awareness, hidden addictions or compulsions may guide leaders to behaviors that create huge problems and may dismay, exasperate, and bewilder those they lead."[2]

Becoming aware of yourself sounds like it could lead to being self-absorbed, but the opposite should actually be true. To be self-aware will require the input of others. If leaders establish a level of self-awareness, they can use that insight to acknowledge strengths and weaknesses, help others address their issues, develop a team to compliment their strengths, and take specific steps to improve weaknesses. Usually leaders who are unaware of their true nature, habits, and shortcomings are the ones that drive people crazy and damage their leadership credibility.

Here are some practical questions that can help you get started discovering the real you:

1. How did your family influence the person that you are? What traits and habits did you learn from your family situation growing up, both good and bad?
2. Who could you ask to give you some honest feedback on ways that you interact positively with people? Who can give you some feedback on ways that you, well, act like a jerk or an idiot?
3. Do you have any habits that rule your time and energy in an excessive way? You will need to ask those around you.
4. When is the last time you studied how you actually use your time? Could you track your time for a week in fifteen- or thirty-minute segments?
5. Do you know how to say "Yes" to the right things and "No" to some things that may be good but may not be what is best for you to be doing?
6. Which of these words best describes how you normally respond to conflict—avoidance, withdrawal, yield, fight-to-win, or loving confrontation?
7. When is the last time you felt encouraged? When is the last time you encouraged someone else?

While not a complete list, these can be used to develop self-awareness. Leaders who are unwilling to work on self-awareness can end up being shallow or egotistical. Those leaders will likely lose credibility and be unable to develop good relational connections, especially with the younger generation.

Vulnerability

After putting some self-awareness in the mix, the next ingredient has to be added before the rest of the ingredients. If you don't mix in some vulnerability, then others will not have the opportunity to relate to who you really are. This means that you are willing to open the window and let others look into your soul, at least occasionally. It doesn't mean that you have to run around wearing everything "on our sleeve" all the time.

However, a touch of vulnerability does require the willingness to take a risk. It can be dangerous to let others see who you really are. They might not like what they see. On the other hand, some people have probably seen glimpses of your shortcomings and strengths, whether you think they are hidden or not. Most of the time we are the ones fooling ourselves into thinking that nobody ever notices when we are being an idiot or do something good.

People are watching; they are especially watching leaders. One of the leaders from Threads Church in Portage, Michigan, describes the importance of leadership transparency and vulnerability this way in regard to reaching the younger generation:

> As I read through the Bible, it is just so raw in so many places. If we are simply honest about that, that in itself is real. And then, if we are pursuing honest relationships with one another in community with each other, that's real. And those things, on their own, don't have any pretense.
>
> But if we begin to have a pretense where it is perceived as some kind of contrived marketing gimmick, unchurched people will just sort of see that and sort of shy away, you know because we have had so many unchurched people, we're actually sensitive to that and aware of that because they are looking. When they say that they mean that and they don't want . . . they don't need gimmicks. And they are not looking for gimmicks.[3]

Being vulnerable will help give people the real thing. They are looking for some raw reality, and that requires vulnerability.

Careful Honesty

Once leaders have combined self-awareness with a little bit of vulnerability, it will be time for them to add in some careful honesty. Notice, we are discussing more than honesty; we are mixing in *careful* honesty. That distinction is very important. In other words, it's really essential to be concerned about how you share what you share.

Careful implies paying close attention to what you say. Careful means that you express great concern for your own work and responsibilities, as well as what is important to others. Careful honesty means that you are willing to share openly, look people in the eye, and answer the tough questions. But at the same time, that requires guarding against injuring yourself or others with the truth. It's not always an easy balance to maintain.

In Ephesians 4:14–15 the apostle Paul had something to say about this issue of careful honesty—"Then we will no longer be little children, tossed by the waves and blown around by every wind of teaching, by human cunning with cleverness in the techniques of deceit. But speaking the truth in love, let us grow in every way into Him who is the Head—Christ" (HCSB). If we can engage in self-awareness, are vulnerable, and speak the truth in love with God's help, we will better relate to the younger generation. Not only that, but we will also become more like Jesus in the process.

Time

The next ingredient for leading with transparency is time. Or, maybe we should just say that leading the transparent way takes time, but it's worth it.

One of the pastors from Biltmore Baptist Church in Arden, North Carolina, describes the impact their pastor has had by being sensitive to time:

> He is a dynamic preacher and incredible visionary leader.
> But one of the things he does, his messages, while heavily
> biblically based are incredibly focused on reaching people in
> more of a heart sense, reaching out and touching them. And
> just saying, "Listen, I am going to give you biblical truth, but
> I am also going to let you know I care about you and I love
> you."
>
> After every message he preaches, he never leaves the
> auditorium. He reaches out, and he touches people. He will
> sit down and actually spend time with them. But one thing
> that he has shown us, I think, is that people really don't care
> what you have to say as much as they want to know how
> much you care. People are walking around saying, "You know
> what? This guy really cares about us. Not only does he lead
> this church and does he preach, but he cares about me."[4]

Being transparent means taking the time to be available and show real concern. Good pastors, shepherds, and leaders know that it is essential to find the time to walk slowly among the people. Why is that important? Because it is an opportunity to show people that you really care. Maybe taking time for you will involve instant messaging with people late on a weeknight or spending time at the places where people are hanging out. Wherever it is and whenever it is, finding time to be available is crucial.

In addition, building relationships that are transparent takes time. It's not about rolling out the occasional transparent moment, and now we are all friends for life. Younger people want to see that self-awareness, vulnerability, and careful honesty are consistent traits in your life. They want to know that you care about community needs and world issues over the long haul. Just mentioning that AIDS and poverty are important issues every now and then isn't going to make an impact.

Obviously this issue of time is about availability and investment. Are we willing to structure our lives in such a way that we can be available to others in need? Are we willing to invest in people's lives over the long haul, with no strings attached? When building relationships, we have to be less concerned about having an instant return on investment.

Real Excellence

Just like making a gourmet meal, leading with transparency takes time, energy, and resources. If it's going to be gourmet, you can't skimp on the ingredients. It just won't turn out the same way. You can't practice leadership transparency without some self-awareness, vulnerability, careful honesty, and time. One last ingredient to add to the mix is real excellence.

Doing things with excellence is not wrong, unless it's not real. If it's just about putting on a good show, then it's not real excellence. When people practice hard, give their best, and still mess up, it's not the end of the world. We are still fallen human beings; we will make mistakes. (I know this is really hard for you perfectionists out there.) People will forgive the lack of excellence if it is real. However, they will not forgive the lack of real, even if it is excellent!

This has to do with what's more important for younger generations. If you visit Aletheia Church in Harrisonburg, Virginia, it is a church focused on reaching students at James Madison University. They meet in an old warehouse. That is probably not the definition of excellence for most people. They certainly don't dress up for church. But they seek to do several things with excellence—music, technology, graphics, evangelism, and relationships.

Relational Results

When you mix these ingredients (self-awareness, vulnerability, careful honesty, time, and real excellence) together, it produces a transparent and powerful ministry to young adults. Your leading with transparency will be like a breath of fresh air to people who are bombarded every day with false realities and false claims. Being aware of self and the world around you, showing vulnerability, and displaying careful honesty will open the door for people to deeply connect with you and one another.

How Churches Are Leading with Team

IT WAS A STRANGE NEW WORLD. ONE THEY HAD NEVER SEEN before. Sure they had heard many imaginary stories about all the riches and treasures, but honestly, when they stepped ashore, they really didn't know what to expect. After a brief rendezvous in Cuba, Hernán Cortez led his four hundred men to the coast of present-day Mexico. It was winter, but it wasn't cold. The men stepped out onto Mexico's shore in February 1519.

As had been the case in Cuba, a group of men moved to take charge of the now emptied eleven ships. These guys planned to do the normal thing, to guard the ships while Cortez led the rest in exploration of the interior. This was the safe, sensible thing to do. In so doing, there would be a way to escape should Cortez run into a band of head-hunting natives. Who wouldn't want a way to flee if someone was coming down on you with a spear?

Cortez obviously didn't. Before heading inland for a long exploration in search of gold and other treasures, Cortez did something that had never been done before. He ordered his men to burn the ships, thus cutting off any possible avenue for a quick return home. We've all heard the rally cry, "Remember the Alamo." The Alamo cry makes sense, but "Burn the ships"?

History won out. Time marched on. The men fired their torches, and the ships went up in smoke. Now you're wondering, what does this have to do with young adults coming to faith and coming to church? To answer that, we'll have to look at the leadership principle Cortez employed.

In It Together

In the negative sense he was a dictator (and just in case you were wondering, this isn't the kind of leader God is calling us to be). Yet from another angle we can see where Cortez was calling his men to a great and dangerous endeavor. By having the ships put to the torch, Cortez was saying, "We're all in this together." With the ships a distant memory, Cortez might have communicated, "Come on men, we must win and we will win together. Now that the ships are gone, you know I am 100 percent committed to the success of this journey, because I, too, want to go home."

Churches that are effectively influencing young adults highly value an incarnational approach to ministry and leadership. Just as Jesus stepped into this earth He had created so many years ago, God is drawing together teams to abandon all and to serve the greater good for the cause of His kingdom. Like the old hymn, "no turning back, I'll follow Him," there is a great need for surrendered people to leave behind some personal ambition and to join a team that will work together, with the goal of the team being higher and greater than the ambitions of the individual.

When Cortez arrived in the new world, he wasn't looking for options of escape, he arrived with one goal in mind—victory. We too should look at ministry that way. From our research we noticed a trend of great commitment to team in churches that were reaching the young adult world.

Modeling Team

Heeding the call to abandon all and to fashion a team that would mirror the community where they sought to serve, Chad Runge moved with his wife and three young children into a small apartment right smack in the middle of their new mission field in West Ridge (Chicago),

Illinois. By living among the people they were trying to reach, the Runges were able to model community and team.

This was no ordinary living arrangement. The three-bedroom, one-bath unit was shared by Chad's family and another family who had joined together for this new church. Having moved across the country, both families were committed to building a church that would impact the unchurched in their new community.

Chad talked about the importance of the team and its cohesiveness, a common theme expressed by others during our study:

> I can't *not* be open with anybody. If you are going to really
> trust somebody, you are only able to trust as far as you know.
> And so if you are going to model team and if you are going
> to model relinquishing to one another and submitting to
> one another, you are really going to have to die to yourself.
> And you are going to have to look at different aspects and
> moments and say, "You know what? We are struggling here."
> Ministry can be a huge struggle. Many guys I know who
> have struck out on their own in lone-ranger situations have
> had to fight through those struggles alone. They had burned
> the ships, but they didn't have someone walking alongside of
> them in the wilderness reminding them of the mission, taking
> free time to just hang, encouraging them on the dark days, or
> assisting them in creating and recrafting strategies.[1]

Chad's dream, the dream for The Church in West Ridge, was to be an authentic community of faith that impacted the community. Chad would be calling on his people to model community, to really make an impact in the day-to-day lives of those they sought to win to the Lord. Chad told me, "It's not just a pipe dream that you see as pretty cool and hip right now to be a Christian . . . and be in community. If you are really going to see it happen you have got to model it."

In a tight apartment, shared by families who had joined together to model community for the foundation of a new church, a war of sorts would rage. No, don't rush to judgment . . . you remember what it was like to be single and sharing an 11-by-11 cubicle called a dorm room, don't you? And I'm sure you remember leaving that dorm many times just to get away from your roommate?

Chad's team experienced those same emotions. Yet their experience was compounded by the fact that they were two families living under one roof. Chad told me about that experience:

We came to the point where we just couldn't stand each other. I mean, they were ready to move back to Florida, and we were ready to send them. We had to sit down and talk it out. And we had to look at each other and say, "You know me now more than anybody could ever know me. And you are still here. And so we are not going anywhere."[2]

Chad laid out his point:

That's how our leadership is going to work, that is how anybody who is going to lead a small group is going to work. That is just how it works because greater love has no one than this when they lay down their life for their friend. And we see [how in] Acts they had all things in common. We want to be a New Testament, Spirit-empowered church.[3]

From what we see in our research, churches that were led by teams were much more effective in ministering and transforming their communities. I'm not talking about "team" in the sense of a dream team of individually minded, expert staff members calling themselves a team and not living it. I'm referring to "team" in the very real sense of a group of individuals coming together to form an authentic group of friends who would do life together, live in transparency with one another, and work together to make the dream a reality.

These are people who would make their life all about serving their heavenly Father in an incarnational manner moving into a team to be the team . . . moving into a community to be a part of that community and to win that community for Christ. Too often our experience in professional church ministry is more like the model we see in corporate America, where staff is reaching for the next rung on the ladder of success. A team is a group of individuals who've burned the ships on their own agenda. They have bought into the dream and are fully invested in the mission.

Building Team

Building a team can be tricky. The older model of hiring a bunch of experts and asking people to follow them is still very prevalent. Yet building a fully functioning team is worth the effort. Our research reveals that a staff that functions as a team is much more likely to stay together for the long term.

Will you make mistakes as you work to build a team? Probably. Just like the guys who will be on your team, you are, after all, human. Dr. Mike Ladra of First Presbyterian in Salinas, California, turned a dying church around in a remarkable fashion. One of the key elements to his church's success was the team that he surrounded himself with. However there were times when Dr. Ladra discovered his picks for team didn't always make good team members. "We made some mistakes [in] hiring," said Ladra. "The whole church was growing until [we hired] this one pastor and he turned out to be negative." After the new staff member began reversing the growth in his department, moving people away from the church rather than to it, Dr. Ladra had to come to the difficult decision to let him go.

What did Ladra learn from this? Ladra replied, "You cannot be any better than your staff."

Moving staff from expert mode to team mode is critical. Thom Rainer and Eric Geiger show in their book *Simple Church* that churches staffed by experts who do their own thing in their own departments aren't as effective as churches that cultivate a team spirit among their staff. Team doesn't just happen. It is intentional and it is cultivated.

When a church can realize this lesson and move to a more authentic team that models doing life together, then the people will get it. When they get it, they will be motivated to live it and to make an impact on their unchurched community by finding others to do life with them. Then by default, your team will be expanded to a mass of volunteers who have burned their own ships of living out their faith as an island to themselves. Such a church is an empowered church. Such a church is a released church. Such a church is a church that is making the difference in the community, with an incarnational approach, much as Jesus took two thousand years ago when He became flesh and made His dwelling among us.[4]

I'm sure you would agree . . . I would have flipped out (on the inside) if I were one of Cortez's men watching my way home go up in smoke. As the image slowly disappeared, as I followed my leader into the untamed wilderness, I would have had a choice to make. Would I run away and try to make my own life in the wilderness alone, or would I let my heart join the hearts of four hundred others as they followed Cortez?

Team. That's what it is all about. Cortez was ruthless, and history has recorded the atrocities he committed against the natives of Central America. But one thing we know about Cortez (besides that he was

crazy with greed for Aztec gold) is that he knew he would not realize
his dreams without his team of soldiers covering his back. In a similar
way, the pastor must realize his dependence upon his team. He must
realize how much the dream God gives him is tied to the team God
gives him.

Mike Ladra at First Presbyterian spoke to this need of
interdependence:

> I just feel the senior pastor has to develop a lot of humility,
> be teachable by his staff, be an example, and he has to be a
> strong leader. He knows where he is going [and he must] keep
> his staff on vision. There has to be accountability in the staff
> or we [will] always keep saying that the 20 percent produces
> 80 percent of the results. So I do insist that we [the team of
> staff] be doing the right things. So there is strong leadership
> and vision, and yet there is this camaraderie and invitation to
> be creative, I think, is that's why our staff is long term.[5]

How will you revisit your concept of team? How might you invite
your staff to revisit this concept with you and even to give you their
input? Don't be afraid, light the match and burn the ships, together.
Then, go ahead, bust a move, and sing, "We're all in this together."
I can assure you that at my house we sing a lot of this tune.

Part 3 Wrap-Up

1. Young adults are trying to connect and will make a lasting connection wherever they can find belonging. Churches that are effective at reaching and developing young adults place a high value on community and are using small groups to build that community.

2. Young adults want to be a part of something bigger than themselves and are looking to be a part of an organization where they can make a difference through acts of service. More than ever before, young adults are thinking locally and globally about how they can make a lasting impact. Churches that are reaching young adults are successful in providing opportunities for service.

3. More than looking for a good performance, young adults desire to connect with the experience of worship. They embrace the future and the past at the same time. Young adults want to be challenged by the message, and they want to participate in a worship experience.

4. Young adults are looking to move behind the trite and into more depth—and we found this among the churched and unchurched young adults.

5. Many churches are waking up to the need to embrace technology as an effective tool in reaching the unchurched.

6. Young adults need cross-generational relationships. Churches that are linking young adults with older, mature adults are challenging young adults to move on to maturity through friendship, wisdom, and support.

7. Young adults are looking for and connecting to churches where they see leaders that are authentic, transparent, and on a learning journey.

8. Young people are desperately seeking something real, something authentic—and they don't mind if it is messy. One hundred percent of churches reaching young adults hold authenticity as one of their highest values.

9. Team is an often desired but infrequently lived value. Churches that lead by teams—and invite young adults to be a part of those teams—engage all kinds of people in more effective mission and ministry.

Conclusion

WE HAVE LOOKED AT RESEARCH OF WHO YOUNG ADULTS ARE, the four pillars of young adult ministry, and nine trends in churches that are reaching young adults.

Churches seeking to engage young adults do so at a crucial and opportune time. If we will unapologetically seize the opportunity for effective ministry, the opportunity is great. But this is not just an opportunity for our churches to grow and for our denominations to survive, but rather this is about an opportunity for those we've been discussing—young adults. Their opportunity is to discover the greatness of God for themselves and to explore His plan for not only this time of their life, but for all of eternity.

The potential of this generation is hard to fathom. If we can connect them to God and the church, the world could truly be changed forever. Rather than looking toward young adults as a burdensome challenge, let us look at them with hope and potential. We could have written an entire other book about the amazing things young adults are currently doing for the kingdom. We can be excited about both churched young adults and also the possibilities that exist for those who are currently unchurched. If the passion, intellect, and talents of this generation could be connected to the mission of God, then a great revival would invade our local communities and stretch far beyond our North American churches.

Finally, let us never lose sight of the amazing good news that we have in Jesus. Although we need to be wise and discerning in how we strategize our ministries and structure our churches, it's important we remember how empty our efforts are without the atoning work of Jesus and the continual presence of the Holy Spirit. We hope that this book has not led you toward a prescriptive set of answers, but rather it's caused you to evaluate your ministry in new ways and actually ask some important questions. It's not for us to tell you how your ministries should look. We trust you will seek the Lord in what that looks like for you. But be encouraged. As we've shown in this book, young adults are seeking the very things that one can find in a walk with God. It's our responsibility to accurately reflect His character in our personal lives and our churches. As that happens, I believe this generation will begin to turn toward God, and, as a result, reacquaint themselves to the church.

— THE LOST AND FOUND STORY CONCLUSION —

Mitch had to admit it: That was truly one of the best sets Aaron had ever played, and now he was over there with his Stratocaster soaking up the audience's applause. Mitch knew how insufferable Aaron was on nights he didn't play half this well. He couldn't imagine what it would be like during the break.

As the applause continued and Mitch lifted the guitar strap from over his shoulder, he wondered again, "God, why isn't Aaron a Christian? When I think about the challenges with where Ally, Dean, and Jacob are spiritually, I can at least concede they have some major issues to overcome with God, the church, and especially Christians. Man, they've got a lot of baggage about Christians. But what gives with Aaron?"

Mitch thought about the ground he and Aaron had covered in six years. He'd known Aaron longer than any of his other friends and honestly couldn't point to any major spiritual shift in Aaron's life since they'd known each other. He and Aaron hit it off immediately that day they moved into the dorm and Mitch followed the guitar sound up a stairwell and down a hall to see Aaron sitting on an amp and jamming. They wound up playing for hours that day then grabbed a bite to eat.

"Where'd you learn to play that well?" Mitch had asked.

"Honestly, most of it was listening to music and figuring it out. I learned some fingering from this Mel Bay DVD I bought off eBay, then just spent hours playing. How 'bout you? That's some pretty good bass playing."

"Actually, guitar is what I learned first," said Mitch. "There's a guy at my church who plays in our church band. Awesome guitar player; a really in-demand studio player. It's what he does for a living. Guy's name is James. You need to meet him sometime. I started lessons with him when I was sixteen. The bass player got a job transfer and they needed somebody. By that time I'd been playing a couple years and switched pretty easily."

Aaron and Mitch spent hours together just jamming—maybe too much time. They eventually found a drummer and a rhythm guitar player. Mitch just knew Aaron would be all over meeting James, and he thought the best way to do that was to invite him to church so he could see James play, then spend some time talking afterwards. To his surprise, Aaron wasn't big on going. He couldn't figure out why. In the hours they'd spent together, they talked about everything under the sun, from guitars and music to theology and life. Aaron had met Mitch's family and Mitch had even gone home one weekend with Aaron.

But every time he brought up church, Aaron was ambivalent. On the way to supper one night, Mitch just asked.

"Dude, what gives on church?"

"What do you mean?" Aaron asked.

"I've asked you to go to church a number of times and you're pretty cool on it. I thought you'd be all over it. To meet James if for no other reason. I mean we've done a lot of God talk and you believe in one God, you believe Christianity is relevant to life, you've grown up going to church, you've even come to some of the small groups I've led here in the dorm. What gives on the church thing?"

"Honestly," Aaron started, "I don't need it. Like you said, I believe in God. I don't need a church telling me what I should and shouldn't believe. I mean seriously, I get a spiritual experience playing music and knowing God created music. I believe He gave me the gift to play. When I'm playing I feel connected to Him. How is the church going to improve on that? Besides, growing up I never felt like the people at church were real. Everybody seemed plastic. Now that I've got a choice about going, I got no interest in that."

Mitch didn't know where to go with that. He really couldn't argue with Aaron's point about authenticity at church. The place his family went *before starting at his current church was pretty plastic. But how could he convince Aaron his church was different. He talked to James to see if he had any ideas.*

"Stick with him and keep inviting him," he said. "Don't irritate him, but challenge him on it. Ask him how he can pass judgment on all churches based on the experience he had at a single church a few years ago."

That made perfect sense to Mitch. How could Aaron claim to be open-minded yet be closed-minded about this?

That was six years ago. Mitch was truly grateful for the dozen or so times over these past six years Aaron had gone to church with him, for the many spiritual conversations the two had had and all the small group studies Aaron attended. But the church thing was still a hang-up for Aaron.

"Of course," Mitch thought. "The objective is not to get him into church attendance but see him get into a relationship with Christ."

As Mitch walked down the steps toward the "friends" table, he thought about this little band of people in which he'd invested so much time. These truly were friends. He loved them. He'd walked through life with them. He prayed for them and he'd presented the gospel to every one of them. How he deeply wanted to see each of them put their faith in Jesus. At times it was discouraging but James reminded him salvation belongs to God.

"Mitch, you weren't called to save these people," James counseled not too long ago. "You were called to persevere with these people. They haven't quit on you. Don't you quit on them."

James's words echoed in his head as he reached his friends.

"He's right, God, and only You know what tomorrow will bring."

NOTES

Introduction

1. Robert Wuthnow, *After the Baby Boomers* (Princeton University Press, 2007), 69.
2. Ibid., 135.

Chapter 2

1. The Center for Missional Research (CMR) at the North American Mission Board (NAMB) surveyed the nine hundred unchurched young adults from ages twenty to twenty-nine. LifeWay Research interviewed an additional 502 unchurched Americans age thirty and over for comparison. LifeWay Research also re-asked several questions for more clarity. By combining the 1,402 interviews, it is possible to learn much about the views and beliefs of the unchurched in America and make comparisons between generations as well as other key demographic groups. Zogby International, Inc., of Utica, New York, conducted both telephone surveys. Researchers and theologians have defined unchurched differently over the years. The screening question for this study was "Have you attended a religious service in a church, synagogue, or mosque, other than for a religious holiday, or for special events such as a wedding or funeral, at any time in the past six months?" The two samples were combined by weighting them statistically to the age group population of the United States. The resulting sampling error would not be expected to exceed ±2.5 percent.

2. American Community Survey, 2006. U.S. Bureau of the Census.

3. Dan Kimball, *They Like Jesus but Not the Church* (Grand Rapids, MI: Zondervan, 2007).

Chapter 3

1. Because of sampling statistics for the two surveys, differences between the two age groups of less than 10 percentage points on any one item may not provide overwhelming statistical significance. However, the fact that *all* of the measures are tilted in the same direction is evidence that younger folks hold stronger beliefs about God.

Chapter 4

1. A study of unchurched Americans conducted by LifeWay Research in partnership with the North American Mission Board's Center for Missional Research.

2. Descriptions of various types of community were adapted from Wikipedia (http://en.wikipedia.org/wiki/Community).

3. "The Third Place" adapted from Wikipedia (http://en.wikipedia.org/wiki/Starbucks).

4. LifeWay Young Adults Research Project.

5. Material adapted from McLean Bible Church at www.mcleanbible.org/pages/page.asp?page_id=15901.

Chapter 5

1. John Calvin, *Institutes of the Christian Religion* (Grand Rapids, MI: Baker Academic, 1987), 35.

2. Michael Kelley quote taken from www.threadsmedia.com/index.php?/staff_blog/blog_post/we_like_things_tough.

3. Interview with Michael Kelley. Many of the same sentiments are expressed in his book, *Tough Sayings of Jesus II* (Nashville, TN: LifeWay Church Resources, 2007).

4. Quote from Eugene Peterson; source unknown.

5. Ralph Waldo Emerson quote taken from http://thinkexist.com/quotation/it_is_not_length_of_life-but_depth_of_life/225077.html.

6. This quote was submitted by Margaret Feinberg for this book on the topic per our request.

Chapter 7

1. See http://threadsmedia.com/lead/article/sherpas-mentors-and-intergenerational-ministry.

2. Sam and Robyn live in Knoxville, Tennessee. Sam has mentored Jason for many years.

Chapter 8

1. See http://quixpins.blogspot.com/2006/07/cult-like-cultures.html, Feb. 14, 2006.
2. See http://blog.guykawasaki.com/2006/02/the_art_of_crea.html.
3. Interview with Steve Derdowski, senior pastor at Ambassador Church in Littleton, Colorado.
4. Interview with Danny Parmelee of Epikos Church in Milwaukee, Wisconsin.

Chapter 9

1. Interview with Kevin Marsico at Northstar Community Church in Monrovia, Maryland.
2. Interview with Brad Edwards, pastor of adults at Cherry Hills Community Church in Highlands Ranch, Colorado.

Chapter 10

1. Interview with Mike Ladra, senior pastor at First Presbyterian Church in Salinas, California.
2. Interview with Dave Fergusion, lead pastor at Community Christian Church in Naperville, Illinois.
3. Ibid.
4. Interview with Matt Fry, senior pastor at C3 Church in Clayton, North Carolina.
5. Interview with Ed Emmerling, pastor at Westside Baptist Church in Flushing, Wisconsin.

Chapter 11

1. Interview with Marty Mosher, pastor at The Fellowship at Plum Creek in Kyle, Texas.
2. Interview with Matt Fry, senior pastor at C3 Church in Clayton, North Carolina.
3. Ibid.
4 . E-mail correspondence between Ed Stetzer and Mark Driscoll, pastor at Mars Hill Church in Seattle, Washington.
5. Quote from survey with Mark Lenz, campus pastor to groups at the multi-site Eagle Brook Church, Spring Lake Park Campus in Spring Lake Park, Minnesota.

Chapter 12

1. Interview with Jason Wilson, executive pastor at New Spring Community Church in Anderson, South Carolina.
2. See http://www.startribune.com/lifestyle/faith/25636704.html?location_refer=Homepage:latestNews:4.

Chapter 13

1. Interview with Beau Adams, senior pastor at Community Bible Church in Stockbridge, California.

Chapter 14

1. Patrick Lencioni, *The Five Dysfunctions of a Team* (San Francisco, CA: Jossey-Bass, 2002).
2. See www.Dictionary.com.
3. E-mail to Ed Stetzer from Matt Chandler, pastor at The Village Church in Highland Village, Texas.
4. Interview with Chad Runge, senior pastor at The Church in West Ridge (Chicago), Illinois.
5. Ibid.
6. Interview with Greg Byman, senior pastor at St. Joe Community Church in Fort Wayne, Indiana.
7. See www.henrinouwen.org/henri/about.
8. Interview with Peter Ahn, senior pastor at Metro Community Church in Fort Lee, New Jersey.

Chapter 15

1. Interview with pastor at Riverpoint Church in Newton, Kansas.
2. Reggie McNeal, *Practicing Greatness: 7 Disciplines of Extraordinary Leaders* (San Francisco, CA: Jossey-Bass, 2006), 11.
3. Interview with pastor at Threads Church in Portage, Michigan.
4. Interview with one of the pastors at Biltmore Baptist Church in Arden, North Carolina.

Chapter 16

1. Interview with Chad Runge on the mission field in West Ridge (Chicago), Illinois.
2. Ibid.
3. Ibid.
4. Thom S. Rainer and Eric Geiger, *Simple Church* (Nashville: B&H Publishing Group, 2007).
5. Interview with Mike Ladra at First Presbyterian in Salinas, California.